Nikki Gemmell's critically acclaimed fiction has been translated into many languages. Her novels include the international bestseller *The Bride Stripped Bare*, *Shiver*, *The Book of Rapture* and *With My Body*. She has written two non-fiction books: *Why You Are Australian* and *Pleasure: An Almanac for the Heart*. Wollongong-born, she was based in London for many years and has now returned with her family to Australia, where she writes a regular column for the *Weekend Australian Magazine*. Visit www.nikkigemmell.com

BY NIKKI GEMMELL

HONESTLY

notes on life

NIKKI GEMMELL

FOURTH ESTATE

Fourth Estate
An imprint of HarperCollins*Publishers*

First published in Australia in 2012
by HarperCollins*Publishers* Australia Pty Limited
ABN 36 009 913 517
harpercollins.com.au

Acknowledgment is made to the *Weekend Australian Magazine*, where many of
these columns were first published.

HarperCollins*Publishers*
Level 13, 201 Elizabeth Street, Sydney NSW 2000
31 View Road, Glenfield, Auckland 0627, New Zealand

National Library of Australia Cataloguing-in-Publication data:
  Gemmell, Nikki.
  Honestly : notes on life / Nikki Gemmell.
  ISBN 978 0 7322 9589 9 (pbk.)
  ISBN 978 1 7430 9733 5 (ebook : epub)
A823.3

Cover design by Darren Holt, HarperCollins Design Studio
Cover photograph by Sue Daniel
Typeset in Adobe Garamond Regular by Kirby Jones
Printed and bound in Australia by Griffin Press
The papers used by HarperCollins in the manufacture of this book are a natural,
recyclable product made from wood grown in sustainable plantation forests.
The fibre source and manufacturing processes meet recognised international
environmental standards, and carry certification.

6 5 4 3 2 1   12 13 14 15

Contents

Introduction

So here it is, dear reader. A jostling, an exuberance, a provocation, a tumble and a tease of columns, all from the *Weekend Australian*. But wait, there's more! Some extra essays, just for this book, because I couldn't resist. Plus some expansions on the most popular columns – those most requested weeks, months later – because frankly I'm always chafing at the bit with the pinch of *The Oz*'s rigorous word limit and seized the chance to write more, more!

What becomes a columnist most? For me, it's uncertainty. Hallam Walker Davis wrote in his journalism handbook of 1926, *The Column*: 'there is one good thing that all columns have, and have in abundance. That thing is the "individuality" or "personality" or "ego" of the columnist. If this indefinable thing is pleasing and positive and challenging, the column's success is assured'. Yet with me, I feel my work's marked by bewilderment, vulnerability, as much as anything. I write to understand. It feels like there's a lot of questioning and frustration in Australia right now; that the voice of regular people is often not being articulated, is being drowned out by the shouters, the affronted, the haters, the furious. My columns are making a stand against all that, presenting another way. Turning things upside down and shaking them, sometimes vigorously; but with decorum and soul and let's just say gentle probings rather than rants. Max Harris, writing in the '60s and early '70s, described a columnist's role as 'trying to define what is happening in the Australian ethos at any given moment, and in establishing what it means … The columnist's job is to see the wood despite the daily trees.'

My mantra is E.M. Forster's epigram: 'Only connect.' Not with sneer or rage or putdowns, but with honesty. Most of all that. There's no shying away from my own weaknesses, embarrassments, confusion, because I've learnt that it's a way of connecting, powerfully, with the reader. I found with my own fiction – *The Bride Stripped Bare* and *With My Body* in particular – that telling the truth can be enormously liberating, viscerally aligning. I want my words to be remembered, tussled with, lingered over, tucked in the journal and the heart. And because by trade I'm a novelist who aspires to have a unique writing voice and who uses poetry as her tuning fork, there must be beauty too. So a novelist's shaping, honing, crafting, goes into these weekly offerings. And the aim with all my work is audacity, above all. Daring. A few hours' toil with both fiction and non-fiction can leave me feeling like I've run a marathon: the shoulders are aching, the mind's depleted, drained. But I wouldn't want to be doing anything else.

The tradition of the columnist, stretching back to the mid 19th century, is to be cheeky, vigorous, splenetic, irreverent, sometimes even going against the editorial grain of the institution that so graciously, generously carries you. Oh yes, I've filed more than once with heart in mouth, thinking, 'Well, this is it. It was great while it lasted.' But never once have the powers that be at *The Oz* demanded changes, and only occasionally does my saintly magazine editor, Christine Middap, suggest softenings or tweaks. Rather than echoing the official voice of the newspaper, I stand alongside it; dare I say, at times, counter to it. Here's to a robust plurality of opinion, and being given the space to express it! Readers often express their astonishment, 'and in *The Australian* of all places.' It makes me laugh. I do wonder how long I can get away with it.

The start of every week is held hostage to the deadline. So, *what* will it be about this week? It was easy at first but is becoming more challenging, as the months gallop on, to be consistently fresh yet varied. Every Sunday night there's a little clench of anxiety as a topic starts to float to the surface, harden. Monday's a rush of words and researching, sometimes involving a dive back into 30 years' worth of notebooks as that elusive quote written down somewhere in the late teens, the twenties, is retrieved. Or perhaps not. Deadline looming, I've got to crack on. A skeleton of a piece firms in the laptop, usually about twice the required word length, is fleshed out, rearranged, then comes the honing. Again and again, brutally. So many words tossed out!

The aim is to have the piece done and dusted by Monday night, but more often than not Tuesday morning's spent on final polishing then filing – and oh, the blessed relief of the send button. Free! Because then my mind can uncurl, can dwell within the novelist's world of dreaming and shaping and creating. It's a very different world: one that's needy, sensitive, greedy; it demands a lot of thinking time. I took on the non-fiction gig with *The Australian* under strict instructions to self that this new way of being mustn't bleed too heavily into the fiction domain. Still working on that bit. Sometimes, come Wednesday, I just have to tumble into bed at midday because I'm so buggered (did I mention there are four kids in the mix, also?).

A dream, on occasion, is of Jeffrey Barnard's famous excuse in *The Spectator* when four simple words signalled, yet again, his column's absence: 'Jeffrey Bernard is unwell.' Bob Considine wrote an entire column in 1973 that consisted of: 'I have nothing to say today.' Well, I don't quite have the confidence to do that, suspect it wouldn't be allowed, and haven't quite run out of ideas yet. But all suggestions are most welcome. Often a piece is sparked at the school gate; mates or the headmistress will say, 'I've got a column for you,' and off they'll go, all of us throwing in our two bob's worth, me digging into the handbag for a docket or a parking ticket to scribble notes down before it all slips away. I hugely appreciate readers' suggestions; some of them – on difficult mothers, on bratty kids – have been the flint that sparks a flame that becomes a column. I love engaging with *The Australian*'s readers, except the haters. (Note to the sour-spirited: you're the ones usually ignored. I just don't read you and, despite what you want, I'm not going to stop writing.) But for the vast majority of people who take advantage of that email address at the bottom of my weekly piece, I'm so grateful for the tips, musings, affirmations and ideas you give me with such graciousness and generosity. Even when you disagree with something I've written, if you do it civilly, I'll always listen. And perhaps even get an article out of it.

My esteemed stablemate Phillip Adams said once that the columnist is writing for an audience and a deadline – not for eternity. But I beg to differ. I'm writing these pieces for that ultimate accolade: the fridge door. Or something similar. Nothing more, nothing less. Or as one reader wrote:

'You, Nikki Gemmell, have made it to our toilet wall ... ! Yes, it's the "pool room" of our "castle" where our treasures are displayed for all to share. Our pin board there contains poems by Kipling, Max Ehrmann, motivational sayings, humour, nonsense and things of note. Your column "Be brave, boys!" hangs in pride of place for my three sons to glean some wisdom from ... and it seems they have. When I commented on my 20-year-old's mature response to a recent family issue, he simply replied "I'm being brave, Mum," and

"You should write to her and tell her." I thought you should know that.'

Music to a columnist's ears! The piece in question, on raising boys, resulted in one of the largest mailbags I've ever received, alongside its companion piece about being a godmother to a new baby girl. When the gift of this book project came along I seized the opportunity to rework and expand both columns. They conclude this collection.

Feel free to rip them out. Nothing would make me happier.

Columns

The long way home

I'm back. For good. From England, which is such a crowded, aggressive, uncertain land to live in – uncertain about where it's going and what it's become.

So, after 14 years, I've washed that land right out of my hair. The whole family has, and as new arrivals in Oz all I can say is: we're getting into it like a showbag.

'It's a pure question of weather,' wrote that wise Antipodean, Katherine Mansfield, in London almost a century ago. Ah yes, the weather. Every year the English winters were becoming harder to bear. It felt like the cold had curled up in my bones and could never be scraped out; my marrow was screaming for sun and I'd lost that lovely Aussie habit of smiling when I talk – it was the wan light, I think, that did it.

There was also the matter of three Pommy tin-lids who insisted stars only happen in DVDs and pools only happen indoors. Coupled with an austere Britain grimming down, the weight of overcrowding, a stretched public service and a mummy saying words she shouldn't, too often, in a life consisting of seemingly little else but a school run twice a day across three clogged London suburbs – who wouldn't flee? It wasn't an optimistic place to raise kids anymore, but an anxious one. Handbags were always tight beside you, tube carriages scanned for suspicious-looking backpacks, sirens incessant. The recent riots have been brewing for a long time now, a year at least; the aggression and anger in the streets was palpable.

And now: rescued by a looser, lighter life. In a little pocket of seaside Australia with a kookaburra on top of the Hills Hoist and neighbourhood kids zooming through houses; the whole blissful Aussie childhood I thought long lost. The pale little Londoners have slipped into it like dirty mugs into a dishwasher. We gaze up at the stretched glory of the starry night and I point out the mighty Southern Cross and get a little teary, I must admit, then they're tumbling into bed exhausted from running about in all the fresh air and sunshine – that's growing them tall, that's honey-ing them up – and I wonder why on Earth it took us so long to come back.

London stole my optimism, Australia has restored it. I feel like I'm being marinated in a sense of belonging, something I fought tooth and nail against in the younger, wilder years. But I need it as I age. Returning is about the serenity and stillness that comes from being part of a deeply known world; the ease of it. My husband and I spent years being outsiders in foreign lands and revelling in that status; but my God, the relief, now, of belonging. It's hitting us like a long cool drink after a sweltering summer's day. I had to leave Australia to reclaim Australia; to see it with new eyes.

So who am I? Former 'Gong girl, Sydneysider, Northern Territorian, novelist and now – just – mum of four; the latest addition so newly minted he's still unnamed. The monikers we loved so much in Britain (Cosmo, Milo, Holden) just aren't working in Oz for some reason …

So here's to the solace of familiarity; the thrumming, throat-swelling joy at being back. England, stimulating, yes – but my heart is held hostage by the Great Southern Land. In exile I learnt one searing thing: life is about wringing the most happiness we can out of our time on Earth, and for me that means old mates and family and land and beauty – a spiky, prickly, ravishing Australian beauty, not that soft, benign, European one. Under a replenishing sun. Right now I'm like a plant turning towards the light, drinking it up. I've found my place in the world, blazing contentment and revelling in the gift of belonging – and of growing up.

It's called home.

(Originally published in the *Weekend Australian Magazine*, 20 August 2011)

Blissfully out of range

The chap, the long-suffering chap in my life, despairs. For years he has been trying to drag me into the 21st century. Countless birthdays I've been presented with various devices aimed at keeping me in touch with him – and the world. The latest shiny gift in its sweet, sweet box: an iPhone.

It makes a great alarm. That's all it's used for. The chap has just about given up on me. You see, despite his propensity for tweed jackets, leather slippers and P.G. Wodehouse, even he has dived fully and deliciously into the glories of modern communication. (Don't get me started on my romantic 40th birthday lunch. There were three of us in the marriage that Friday: me, him and his BlackBerry.)

I do not 'have' a mobile phone. This is very difficult to explain to schools, children, editors and certain friends – some who get extremely cross indeed. 'How am I meant to communicate with you?' one recently barked. (Well, you could pick up the telephone. Or send an email.) 'But your kids will never, ever get any playdates. We ALL TEXT.' By this point said friend was shouting at me. Without realising.

The reason I don't use one? The older I get, the more I crave serenity. And stillness. And silence. Need them, achingly, to function in this world; get kind of anxious and all-at-sea if I don't have them enough. The mobile is not conducive to any of this. Plus I'd never be able to write with one beside me; all that distraction. I'd constantly be checking messages, needing to reply, fretting about why people weren't answering or returning my calls.

I can't allow too much stress into my life. I cease to function. You see, one morning, one terrible morning, I realised my world was too crowded after receiving three phone calls on the landline just before bundling the kids in the car for the run to two different schools. The calls had held me up, I hadn't managed my own breakfast let alone the ever-present, galvanising lipstick, my head was swamped with impending playdates and book deadlines and I'd had a touch too much wine at a dinner party the night before and then a fractious sleep. Fatal combination.

I crammed squabbling kids in the car, throwing the last of the school bags in behind them, and folded up the stroller. Scrunched it down with my Blunny-booted foot and hauled it into the boot.

It was then I heard a faint squeak.

The stroller was responding. The stroller was responding!?! Oh my God, my God, I rushed it open to find a baby, doubled over, stunned. Trembling, I have never held a child so fiercely, so tightly, in my life. Trembling, I ran my hands over its dear little body and skull. The love. The horror. The guilt.

I quietly took a deep breath and strapped my precious baby in the car seat. 'Why are you shaking, Mummy?' asked my eldest as he watched me drive carefully, so carefully, to school. Again and again, before my eyes, was that vision of a Blunny curtly ramming down the stroller. The sickening heft of it.

I realised from that moment my life was too crazy-busy, and the decks needed clearing. Mobiles have screamed 'added complication' at me ever since. The situation has worked so far. Despite my friend's protestations the world gets through by talking on the landline, emailing, or even, God forbid, sending cards.

And my favourite time in England last year? When the ash cloud in Iceland stopped all flights for several glorious days. We lived in West London's Notting Hill and I didn't realise I lived under the flight path until there were no planes, suddenly, overhead. It felt so odd, unnerving, at first – just a clear, deathly-quiet blue that everyone looked up to and marvelled at. Then gradually, into the silence, the vast sky-silence, leaked God. In that frenetic city it was exhilarating, and hugely calming, to experience.

Favete linguis, declared Horace – 'With silence favour me.' Yes please. And doing without a mobile is all part of that plan.

(Originally published in the *Weekend Australian Magazine*, 27 August 2011)

Hail the drover's wife

Only one person had the Aussie speech therapist Lionel Logue quaking in his boots in *The King's Speech*. The King of England, perhaps? The Queen consort? The Archbishop of Canterbury? Not a bit of it. The missus.

'You're being a coward … Get out there, man!' spluttered the King while Lionel cowered behind a door as his fearsome Myrtle bowled home early from her bridge game.

They make 'em tough, those Aussie chicks. Back then and now. That deliciously steely, no-nonsense archetype holding her own against the blokes goes back a long way in Australian folklore. She's called the Drover's Wife and she's rightly celebrated. Read about her in Henry Lawson's story; gaze at all her sturdy glory in Russell Drysdale's painting or, my favourite depiction, Jeff Carter's wearily beautiful photo. There's also something of her in *My Brilliant Career*'s Sybylla and *Seven Little Australians*' Ju-Ju.

What a gal she is. A specifically Aussie chick. Resilient, outspoken, stoic – and respected for being as assertive as the men.

It's a legacy Aussie females carry with them far from these shores. The scene: London, 1997. Freshly arrived in Blighty, feeling distinctly non-Drover's Wife. Shivering, near broke, unemployed, not sure where my life was going or what I was doing in this place. I'd written a novel about an Aussie chick who jumps in her ute and crosses central Australia in search of her father – and needed it sold.

An old-school publisher's office of meticulous bookcases and cigar-fat pens. A gentleman in a tweed jacket sitting across from me. Did he want to publish my book? God no. He just wanted to examine the odd creature behind it. 'You Australian women are very ... strong ... aren't you?' It was not a compliment. I swear there was a curl of the lip.

'Noooo,' I wanted to scream, 'I feel lost and lonely and a failure as a writer – and cold, bloody cold.' But his disdain was galvanising: I realised I had an archetype to live up to. A fabulously positive, bolshy, gutsy one. I walked out tall despite quaking inside, determined to show just how strong I could be.

Australia being a fertile breeding ground for tenacious women was a reason, earlier this year, to repatriate our family – which includes a feisty daughter who runs rings around the rest of us. From angry, Toff-ruled Blighty the situation looked exhilarating. Thirty per cent of seats in the Australian parliament were held by women. A Sydneysider, for example, was well used to women in power, had experienced six layers of it in fact: a mayor, premier, state governor, prime minister, governor general and queen. That was a lot of chick power to either get used to, despair over – or shrug your shoulders and concede they're the best candidates for the job. Which the majority of Aussies seemed to be doing. Wasn't that the feminist dream?

It felt modern – certainly compared to Britain, where the pollies are being drawn from an increasingly narrow pool. (And where the PM, his deputy and chancellor all went to schools with fees higher than the average wage. It's a huge step back from a grocer's daughter ruling the roost.) This new breed of Aussie women seemed like the modern-day equivalent of the Drover's Wife: women who just rolled up their sleeves and got on with it, often with a wry sense of humour – and without sacrificing their femininity.

But by the time I'd returned home the political situation had shifted – NSW's female premier had gone and Gillard's confidence seemed to have been chipped away at; there was something reduced, too careful, about her. All I can say is: Julia, a lot of Aussie women – and their young daughters – are watching you, whatever their politics. We need to see a bit more of the no-nonsense steel of a Drover's Wife. They don't do crushed. They don't do cowed. Don't lose your fight, girl. There's a glorious Aussie archetype to live up to.

(Originally published in the *Weekend Australian Magazine*, 3 September 2011)

As you give ...

All I want is a bit more equality, OK? With the TV remote, the polishing of the bathroom sink, the 3am baby feeds, the 5am baby feeds, the books pages of newspapers, and sex. Pure and simple.

Which is why it's flattening to read the findings of a recent Family Planning NSW survey. Its findings: that oral sex is now so commonplace among Generation Y women that many believe it's required of them. That young Aussie men 'expect' to receive it.

A delicate question: are these men likely to, er, return the favour? Because let's be blunt, when we're talking oral sex among our youth it's more often girls administering to boys. Half the surveyed women, aged 16 to 25, said they'd sometimes been pressured into giving it. Here's one of them: 'When doing it for the first few times as a young teenager, you feel you must do it to impress the guy you like.' A girl of 16: 'Most people I know that have oral sex only do it because everyone else does, and if you don't, you're frigid.'

Heart, sink. Because I glean not a single drop of empowerment, or control, or pleasure in that statement. I'm with you, girl. I do not think of laugh-out-loud deliciousness or exquisiteness or joy when I think of fellatio. Especially in terms of a teenage girl. To me, it's about as appealing as ironing shirts at midnight. I do not feel strengthened as I'm doing it. Do not feel like it's sex the way I want it. To me it's bleak, demeaning and kind of lonely – anyone could be doing it.

OK! I'm not even going to begin to speak for every woman here. Some girlfriends find it incredibly affirming to give so much pleasure to a man, and good luck to them. But I'm with Iris Murdoch when I think of young girls being expected to do this, and complying just so as not to seem frigid: 'There is nothing like early promiscuous sex for dispelling life's bright mysterious expectations.'

May I gently, pleadingly, suggest a touch more equality here? To engender a little less selfishness perhaps, an encouraging of tenderness; a connection, in the loveliest sense? According to a US study, in some teenage circles oral sex is seen as almost obligatory. Scott, 15: 'Me and my friends don't think of it as a big deal. It's really quick and less serious [than intercourse]. And you don't really have to like a girl.' Ah, so where's the sense of respect here, the cherishing, the acknowledging of an actual individual?

Don't get me wrong, I'm all for curbing the teen pregnancy rate (it's argued in some quarters that encouraging oral sex results in this); all for having young people being more aware of their choices and more empowered to say no. As long as it works both ways. Which brings me back to equality. Which brings me to the flipside of all this. You see, I'm of the firm opinion that cunnilingus is one of the most deliciously transcendent joys available to women; and yes, I'm aware that we can seem equally selfish in demanding it. But do women, enough? Equally?

Thank you, God, for giving us the only organ on the human body devoted purely to exquisite sensation: the clitoris. That tiny little pleasure dome has 8000 nerve endings crammed into it (twice as many as the penis). In Greek mythology, when Zeus and Hera visited the hermaphrodite Tiresias to determine whether it was men or women who experienced more pleasure from sex, Tiresias replied: 'If the sum of love's pleasure adds up to 10, nine parts go to women, only one to men.'

So if feminism is all about equality, are we any closer to a world where young women feel just as comfortable requesting oral sex as boys do? A world where boys feel that administering it is expected of them? The Family Planning NSW survey also found that 82 per cent of young women found oral sex enjoyable and rewarding – I just hope that's because they're getting as good as they give.

(Originally published in the *Weekend Australian Magazine*, 10 September 2011)

Surprise, surprise

The fact is, we were far too old for this baby business. It felt like the whole world was screaming at us that this was so.

The hospital classification: 'geriatric mother'. Friends: shock and horror – not congratulations – at the sight of the growing belly. Tiredness: walloped by it. The big pregnancy-maintenance question: not how to locate the toenails to paint them, but how to disguise the greying hair without flooding the foetus with carcinogens.

Entering the touchy-feely birthing suite during a false alarm at 38 weeks, the chap and I instinctively reached for our spectacles – the lights were too dim. We asked how much the baby weighed 'in the old money', didn't get those newfangled kilo things after so long in Blighty. And most tellingly of all, the new mother in the hospital bed beside me was 25 years younger. Yes, I was the old cracker in the back paddock, a perception not helped when the midwife slapped me on the bum after checking the war wounds, as if she couldn't quite believe it either.

How on Earth had Baby Number Four happened? Number Three had been despairingly hard to coax into existence. As our 40s galloped ever nearer, the chap and I had persistently tried but stubbornly, deflatingly, my period arrived, month after month. There were two miscarriages, two howling canyons of grief, and it was obvious we'd left it too late. Then I tried acupuncture – and bingo, within a month I was pregnant. That was it, we thought. Two shining boys and a gift of a girl. We're done.

And now this. A wee little boy with the most beautiful, slow blink, who as I type is being bounced into stillness in the rocker under my foot. A wee little boy with dark, bright eyes who just gazes at all the madness around him as if he can't quite believe the family he's landed among; who's constantly passed from person to person because so many hands want to hold him, marvel, adore. The complete surprise, the astonishing mistake.

It was because we were relaxed, I think. The chap had finished his London job, I'd just completed a book, we could almost smell the idea of home and were revelling in our twilight London days, doing all those things we'd never done enough of with the sheer effort of being parents of young kids. The last thing we were thinking about was babies. In our, ahem, mid 40s. So I'm intrigued, now, by the vast Industry of Anxiety around conception – a highly lucrative industry. All the panic instilled in women as we career towards the age of reckoning, 35; all the statistics thundered at us and all our money spent; which has the effect of clenching us up at the precise moment when we're not meant to be.

And now, the small, bright wonder of this little man at my feet. Unnamed right up until registration deadline – we'd used up all the favourite boy names with the other two. Everyone was throwing in their two bob's worth, but nothing seemed right. The chap and I rarely agree on anything and he'd confessed his strategy to a mate: 'Nikki thinks up all the weird names – then I come in at the end with the killer sensible one.' Ha! I knew the tactics now. Let the battle commence.

My daughter's teacher buttonholed me the day before registration had to be sent. She'd had enough. She's Cornish, the chap's surname is Cornish, and she knew that wild, spiritual place of shipwrecks and surfboards was one of our favourite holiday destinations. Her suggestion? The old Cornish name for James. Instantly it felt right. With great trepidation I emailed the chap. Held my breath.

'Love it,' came the response. Blessed relief.

Welcome to the world, little Jago (pronounced JAY-go). Or, as we prefer to call you: the Timewaster. Because we can't stop gazing at you, in shock and wonder and absolute delight, at every available moment.

(Originally published in the *Weekend Australian Magazine*, 17 September 2011)

An uplifting download

O brave new world that has such wonders in it! I have seen the future and it is glorious. It's called 'The Fantastic Flying Books of Mr Morris Lessmore'.

Book? Movie? Game? Not sure. All I know is when it was first read/ played/ watched there was a feeling of childlike wonder that made me think of those moments of beauty and innocence when mankind first glimpses the future and is enchanted by it – like when a box in the corner said, 'Good evening and welcome to television.' This feels like the future of reading and as a writer I'm rejoicing; this will save us, I thought. Just experiencing this ... thing ... makes me feel evolved.

It was developed by an American collective of writers, artists and gamers called Moonbot Studios, and they've created something entirely fresh. You download on an iPad what at first seems like a charming tale about the power of books. But I experienced it with my nine-year-old, the Duracell

Bunny – so-called because he never stops bouncing. Reader, he was still. Transfixed. And while Grandma here focused on the text, his fingertip instinctively brought the screen alive – sucked houses into tornadoes, painted skies, played the piano. We roamed it endlessly until, deflatingly, it was finished.

'Mum, where's the next one?'

Music to my ears. Because we were doing something wondrous, together, involving words. You see, this pains me to say it but my nine- and 10-year-old boys do not have Avid Reader hardwired into their DNA. Oh, they'll read, but it's never the staying-up-'til-midnight childhood thing I had. They have to be nudged towards a book. There's the clash and jangle of so many other things, not least the great, insidious march of the screens.

It feels like books, in their conventional form, are dying all around us – certainly in terms of young people. At a school market stall recently a huge pile of tomes languished like wallflowers at a dance. 'No one wants books anymore,' lamented a mum next to me. I used to think that a house without books was like a person without curiosity – unsettling. But more and more now I'm going into homes without any books in them besides cookbooks – that would have killed a friendship once. In the recent UK riots, apparently, all the shops in Clapham High Street were targeted except the bookshop. That's not respect, it's indifference.

My boys are the compact generation. They'll travel the world with their whole life stored in an electronic device:

office, cinema and library in the palm of a hand. I want to make sure that great stories are a part of that. Which is why Moonbot's creation is so exciting, blending hand-drawn animation, digital imagery and, crucially, a compelling narrative. My son and I experienced it together, a rare and lovely thing in this fractured, lonely world of screens. Books were my friends; as a child, they would reach out and take my hand. The Duracell Bunny's hand was held with this.

I feel like I've failed, as a mum, in the book department, so I'm endlessly trying to glean ways to enrapture with words. At the moment we're jumbling together in the loungeroom and reading aloud *Animal Farm*. It feels bizarrely old-fashioned but we're loving it. It's about enchanting and it's the great writers, the enduring ones, who do this best. *Animal Farm* is gripping – as are Shakespeare's narratives. My boys love comics and they've just devoured simplified graphic novels of *Macbeth*, *Lear* and *Henry V*. Strip away the complicated beauty of the language and they're ripping yarns of blood and battles, all those things little boys love. They'll come to the poetry later but for now, slowly but surely, they're developing a love of Shakespeare, of narrative wonder and joy and great, galloping stories, and I'm determined to encourage it. With this generation's kids it feels increasingly vital to be doing this. Thank you, Moonbot, for taking a great leap forward.

(Originally published in the *Weekend Australian Magazine*, 24 September 2011)

You go, girls

There are many beautiful young girls around me at the moment – babysitters, daughters of friends, my own daughter. I look at their vividness, their spark, and want to celebrate it. They seem so bursting with life, articulate and vibrant and bold, so ready to take on the world. Will they?

Author Edith Wharton more than a century ago wrote of 'a curtain of niceness' that befalls young women. It's not necessarily a compliment. It implies a girl who loses her voice as life chips away at her.

There's an interesting paradox going on. Girls statistically are doing better than boys at school, have higher uptake rates at university, leap boldly onto the jobs ladder and damn well climb it, then for an awful lot of us – by our late 30s and 40s – it's all … petered out. Why?

I'm not going to point to motherhood as the entire reason. I think it also has to do with our voice, our confidence, our attitude towards ourselves. I've seen it again and again in newsrooms across Australia and in London. Women who were the workhorses – reliable, smart, hard-working, brilliant – but quiet about it. They never blew their trumpet; they thought someone would recognise how good they were and promote them … but more often than not it never happened. Meanwhile, the bolshy, testosterone-fuelled blokes demanded the glamour jobs – the editorships, the foreign postings – and got them.

Low self-esteem, self-loathing, doubt – they all fell us women. The blokes power on; drowning us out with their loudness. They pick themselves up after the knocks, see it as part of the battle of life. Women take it personally, care enormously, worry so much what people think; it's so easy to crush us.

Sian Westerman is a founding member of the UK's 30% Club, so-called because it wants a minimum 30 per cent women on the boards of all Britain's FTSE-ranked companies. In terms of the older businesses, she says: 'They need to not fall into the trap of thinking that the person who beats their chest the most loudly, the one who is pushing himself forward, is necessarily the best person for the job.'

It's not all rosy in Australia, either. Women in the top echelons of our corporate world are about as rare as a rocking horse poo. The Equal Opportunity for Women in the Workplace Agency has found, over the past 10 years, that more than half the senior executive teams of Australia's top 200 listed companies are female-free. Girls, where are you?

'Oh, can't do that. Oh, not good enough.' Are we our own worst enemy? Actress Carey Mulligan said recently, 'I go to work these days with kind of a "male" attitude. It's not a feminist thing, it just makes me feel more confident. It's my way of feeling like I've got equal weight in the room.'

Equal weight. Because so many of us don't have that attitude at work. Which is why the music world is so exciting at the moment. Look at Lady Gaga, Beyoncé, Adele. There's no vulnerability. Mud doesn't stick. Like Madonna before them, they're not imprisoned by what people think of them – they just roar on. They're empowered, strong, loud; deliciously, cheekily feminine and comfortable in their own skin. It's a killer combination, and right now the chicks are infinitely more interesting – and successful – than their male counterparts in the music world.

Are they blazing the trail for those girls around us at the moment? I watch the gorgeous young women I know in wonder. The spark of them feels so shiny and lovely – I want to protect it, watch it flower. Will it? I hope so. Because what becomes a woman most? Confidence.

(Originally published in the *Weekend Australian Magazine*, 1 October 2011)

Keeping it together

The most important item a woman of a certain age packs on holidays? And by that I'm talking 30s perhaps, definitely 40s, maybe even 20s. A little crucial something that few blokes in their lives will ever even clock? Tweezers.

Not just for eyebrows but, oh, many other nooks and crannies and vast exposed plains that ... let's not go there.

Which leads me to: glamvenience. Those lovely little circuit-breakers in the great cram of life; and as a working mother who often feels like she's failing in thousands of tiny ways, I'm all for them.

A sparkly glamvenience in my recent London life? The department store threading bar, where a wonderful Muslim woman would wield her thread with fingers like knitting needles and pluck my eyebrows into a shape as beautiful as the trail of a falling star, tidying up anything else she could see in the process. I felt restored, because I tell you the eyebrows are starting to go off-piste; some wilfully grey, others thickly curled, and when plucked at home there's likely to be – good grief – a sudden, rogue, bald patch.

Other glamveniences I'd like imported to my neighbourhood right away: Ikea online. Thus avoiding the store entirely. Because the chap and I almost divorced in its aisles once; actually, we almost divorced in the carpark before we got to the aisles.

Topshop To Go. A clothes van would rock up at your home where a gaggle of girlfriends would await; the Tupperware party of modern glamvenience. Mobile computer technicians. Arrive by moped, fix on the spot. Photobox. A cheap digital printing website packaging up photos that make you feel like a pro as you unveil them. Nit salons. Because in London I assumed that headlice was some odd throwback to Dickensian street urchins unique to a city cracking and groaning under the weight of its population.

My new life in Oz? A nit comb, in readiness, at almost every sink. And as older parents – how on Earth do you see the little blighters? The eyesight's failing at a crucial time in our parenthood; we need all the help we can get. Deliverance. A kitchen that delivers restaurant-quality takeaway from all manner of cultures. And Housebites, a website that commissions the nation's best chefs to cook just for you, cut price, and then delivers.

Oh for those latter two! Because right now I'm feeling like the only one in our *MasterChef*-obsessed land who doesn't know how to magic up a soufflé. The splendid dinner parties since arrival – delicious, yes, but everything is so opulent that asking the hosts to one of our own mortifyingly basic kitchen experiences feels far too terrifying. When an old schoolmate said, 'Come for dinner, we'll do takeaway fish and chips,' we were so relieved, we made her a godmother.

Now I know that a lot of these glamveniences are a ridiculously indulgent remedy for those swamping moments of drowning-in-busyness endured by the more pathetic modern types like myself; but sometimes they rescue.

Example: my daughter's recent running carnival. After a morning of dashing all over the place and never quite catching up to where I was meant to be, I staggered onto the playing field, juggling baby capsule and picnic basket. Just as it was ending. Got the time completely wrong. And my girl needs me more than ever right now as she's feeling hugely unsettled by a new baby. The first person I bump into? The crisply-together headmistress. A bemused look on her face. My eyes smarted behind the sunglasses; I could have wept in front of her. I took a photo of my girl, biting my lip to stop the tears flowing. At that moment it felt like the great edifice of calm and control was crumbling all around me – I was crying out silently for all the gods of glamvenience to get me through – but there was no one in sight.

(Originally published in the *Weekend Australian Magazine*, 8 October 2011)

Cool to be kind

It's such a meek little word. Not very fashionable. In some quarters it implies weakness, spinelessness, a lapdog-willingness to please. It seems completely absent from the nation's politics right now. But, my God, the depth-charge of emotion it can stir in the Australian psyche.

It's called kindness.

Think of the resonances around the Gallipoli legend of Simpson transporting wounded comrades on his donkey. The heartbreak in the song 'Two Little Boys' about mates helping each other from nursery to battlefield. The stirring speech on a generous heart in the Aussie cinema hit *Red Dog*. As a girl I remember the extraordinary emotion around Fiona Coote – and when she needed a new heart the Aussies who came forward and said, 'Give her mine.' It was a powerful lesson about sacrifice and selflessness, those words sanctified by grace. During the Queensland floods of January we had 13-year-old Jordan Tyson insisting that his younger brother be rescued first, before being swept to his death.

The older I get the more I respect kindness. Its ability to transform a situation, to soften, move. There's a particularly Australian brand of it. We were flooded by myriad unforgettable kindnesses when we moved back to Oz from England. New to the 'hood, neighbours threw a party to enfold us into the community. When I had the Timewaster, the mums at the boys' school – the little state primary – held a cooking bee (when I gave them all champagne in gratitude I was admonished with 'you big dag' and 'you silly duffer' – things I hadn't been called for 15 years, and God it felt good). Drowning within the exhaustion of new parenthood, a neighbour – all six foot seven of him – arrived one night with gourmet ingredients, cooked up a storm then tenderly held the baby while the chap and I ate. We've been marinated in kindness and it feels peculiarly, movingly Australian.

I'd see it in London a lot. Strapping young Aussie lads breaking all the rules of Tube non-engagement by chatting away to the person beside them. Couches offered to friends of friends; floorspace to store suitcases; dinners and cars. These Aussies felt like teenagers growing too tall, too fast in a grown-up world; sweetly naïve, enthusiastic, kind. In September, in London, Tim Smits became an Aussie hero after getting stabbed while defending women being harassed on a bus. 'I come from a family that taught me good values and to respect people,' he told Britain's media as he recovered.

Respecting people. A basic, life-affirming quality. Perhaps this reckless and spontaneous Aussie kindness developed in the convict days because those in the underclass had to stick together, unite against the bosses, protect each other. Perhaps it arose because this land is so bloody tough; and if we can't help each other out, well, we're buggered. As Professor Stephen Muecke wrote, 'in what other country does the school kid share her musk stick by breaking it and giving her friend the choice?'

It's why the ugliness of a lot of political discourse right now feels so jarring; as if there's a disconnect between people on the ground and those in the public eye; a shocking coarseness. The horrors that the Prime Minister and other powerful women are called on the airwaves – the tone of the voices – is downright ugly and a world away from those sweet, honourable young Aussies who fly the flag for us overseas.

Kindness is about people who are heart-lifters, not heart sinkers. The politics of negativity and sourness is all around us. It feels grubby, reduces us all. Some people think kindness is a weakness but they've got the wrong end of the stick – it's the gift of attention, the highest form of civility. It's about compassion, being a good person. People are drawn to it. Some of our politicians and broadcasters should take note of that.

(Originally published in the *Weekend Australian Magazine*, 15 October 2011)

Nothing compares

Poor old Sinead. Madame O'Connor, of that hauntingly beautiful face, recently blogged that she's desperate for a man – and, more specifically, sex. At the grand old age of 44. Oh, the ironies of womanhood! Just as we enter the age of invisibility, many of us are approaching our sexual prime. We're finally finding a voice.

Example. The misspent youth – late teens, early 20s – involving various ill-matched men whose names I no longer remember. From my side: all about wanting to please. Giving in. Doing things I didn't, actually, want to do. Never having an orgasm. Developing a great line in faking – not only in the understanding of what was meant to be so great about this process; but the fudging at that endless little question, 'So how was it for you?'

Er, not great. But I could never bring myself to say it. It was often bleak and ugly and searingly lonely. Sometimes it hurt. Sometimes I got the feeling that the guys doing things to me didn't like women very much; that they were afraid of them, wanted to chip away at them. 'Only connect,' E.M. Forster wrote in *Howard's End*, but it seemed that with this fundamental human experience there was often a profound, bewildering lack of connection.

This could have been the sum total of my sexual perception. There were huge periods when I just couldn't be bothered. What was all the fuss about? The less sex I had the less I wanted and it was easier that way. Then I found a man who unlocked me, who was determined to find the key to the other side. Reader, I married him.

As I grew older I realised I was far from alone in feeling bewildered during the early years of adulthood; in feeling there must be more to it. I believe now that every woman can be unlocked. That we all have the capacity to be transported into another realm by a sexual experience, to be combusted into light. Catherine Hakim's book *Honey Money: The Power of Erotic Capital* states that women's sexual desire is lower than men's. If that's so, I wonder if it's because a lot of us are living in ignorance. If we've never had a fabulous sexual experience we have no idea what's on the other side. Many men are unaware how to bring a woman truly alive – and many women aren't bold enough to tell them what they really want, and don't.

A recently divorced friend, mid-40s, has just had her first orgasm – with a new boyfriend. Her husband never gave her one (not that he'd know). She's glowing. It reminds me that great sex can flood us with beauty and vividness and spark. 'If our sex life were determined by our first youthful experiments, most of the world would be doomed to celibacy,' P.D. James said. Well, here's to persistence then.

'I only want good sex now,' my mate says. 'I'm too old to stand for anything else.' It's a mantra repeated by many of my girlfriends heading into middle age – and here's to that. We all need help. Marilyn Monroe said, 'I don't think I do it properly.' Me neither, for years. Now I say: go for bold. Do something in bed you've always wanted to, but have never had the courage to ask for. Strip yourself bare; say what you really want. Make love heroically. Act audaciously. A lot of women find it hard to demand sexually. You never know where it'll lead you. Perhaps another – delicious – level entirely.

My friend's learnt to make love audaciously, and that's a big milestone in a woman's sexual life. A lot of us in our younger years can't face the thought of people seeing us as who we really are, for it means losing control of that tight public persona we've so carefully set up. And we never get closer to the truth of our dark, vulnerable, messy selves than with sex. My mate's loosened, relaxed, let go, in the most wonderful way – and it took her until the age of invisibility to get there.

(Originally published in the *Weekend Australian Magazine*, 22 October 2011)

By royal command

She is still. So very still. Amid all the nervous energy and excitement. It defines her. Here, in Buckingham Palace, her house. And beyond it.

The invitation was not so much suggestion as summons. 'The Master of the Household has received Her Majesty's command to invite …' Surreal, magical, impossible. Meeting the Queen with other Australians, in Buck House, on the eve of her Australia tour?

Too busy; the gilt-edged card regretfully put aside. Mentioned in passing to my dad. He said he'd kill me if I didn't go. Debrett's, the authority on etiquette, explained one does not lightly refuse the Queen's command. I could see the shine of it in my parents' faces, my children's; we're programmed to respond to narratives of enchantment, are we not? Come on old cynic, get a move-on. Life is for seizing. So, the baby was bundled up. Flown to London for four mad days. Gulping life, yes, damn well skolling it. What to wear?

The invitation said 'day dress'. How to curtsy – does one? Shake hands? God knows.

Buckingham Palace has masculine hauteur, is sternly fenced off and curiously blank. Perhaps that's the key to its mystique: what on Earth's behind it? Well, slip beyond its gilded railings, look back briefly at the tourists pressing cameras through iron bars, marvel at the sheer unbelievability of it all, then walk through that seemingly impenetrable stone oblong, and lo and behold: a central courtyard. Of astonishing lightness. So, a palace hollowed out, who would have thought? Behind its solid edifice is playfulness, airiness, relief.

And its protector? Caretaker rather than owner. Her home a museum, art gallery, tourist attraction, where someone happens to live. She touches the place lightly. Up the huge staircase, through rooms fat with staff, past walls crowded with paintings. We are announced one by one; a whiff of Shakespeare's histories in the sheer pageantry of it. Occupation, 'author'; title, 'Ms' (the chap won't be liking that). The Queen tiny, much smaller than expected, as is the Duke. Her skin smooth, pale, luminescent, as if it's never seen a wink of sunlight; the wondrous antithesis of elderly Australian women. She's apparently met four million people, I a drop of sand in the duty of her life. It's only when I tell her how gorgeous she looks that she cracks that radiant, girly smile that zooms you back to photos of her as a young woman. 'The strongest argument for doing away with the royal family is … what it reduces us all to,' commentator Polly Toynbee wrote. Well, I'm reduced. For I know I curtsied to the Queen and can still feel the imprint of her brief, firm handshake but cannot explain how I did both. It could be age but I put it down to addled, dazzled wonder. She has that effect.

What's evident, most of all, is containment. Rare poise. The antithesis of modern-day celebrity. 'Aren't they prima donnas?' she reportedly said of footballers to the Premier League chairman. She has a radiant sense of composure. Doesn't do questions. Has been known to greet innocent inquiries such as 'Did you have a nice Christmas?' with a stare.

The Queen embodies solid, old-fashioned qualities of duty, robustness, modesty, endurance, service. British artist Tracey Emin recently installed in the Prime Minister's residence a neon artwork proclaiming 'more passion'. I'd love to see her create an artwork around the Queen. Can't imagine it. By Her Majesty's mystery we are drawn, the composure through so much. This palace bombed seven times during wartime, her father unseemly thrust into the monarchy, half of her realms becoming republics during her reign, blanks fired as she rode, a bedroom intruder, her skittish family. There's something deeply moving about her stillness.

(Originally published in the *Weekend Australian Magazine*, 29 October 2011)

The final curtain

My grandmother died recently. She was 101, and she'd started sleeping a lot; a sign, I've learnt, that the end is near.

Her funeral wishes were beautiful in their austerity, but singular. Just her son and daughter were to be present as she was lowered into her husband's grave at Kurri Kurri. No church, no priest. A tall blue sky above and a bush taut with sound around her. Not her children's loyal spouses, nor any of her grandkids; we were to remember her in our own way. Dad, as the new head of the family, was firm despite protests; we're all close. 'The services aren't what they used to be when they were big community events,' he said. 'It's what she wanted. And none of her friends are left.'

Lexi was a sharp old thing. She did it her way, as she'd done all her life. So as she was being lowered into her grave I was sitting on a jetty with a Thermos of tea, her favourite tipple, and her beloved deco teacup, remembering those old, broad, Hunter Valley vowels. The way she'd call a scourer a 'scratcher'. Movies, 'walkie talkie photos'. The gramma pies. But most of all her lightness as the ageing took hold – and the hooting laughter with it – as if growing old was a process of becoming more light-hearted, and wondrous, at the simple, ravishing beauty of so much around her.

She didn't want an unknown priest. I get that. I've been to funerals where grief is compounded by anger at the seeming indifference of the religious figure before us, as if they're thinking more about the roast dinner ahead than the people around them; an insult I didn't want inflicted on Lexi. I've been angry not only for the person who's passed away, but the church itself. It's a captive audience. Often many in the congregation rarely go to church and this is the moment for the big sell. So, do it! Embrace the mystery of the institution you represent; win us over. We may have read Richard Dawkins but we could, possibly, be partial to a bit of seduction. If your institution is to survive it must engage. It's a vast marketing business, guys. What you're selling is your future, your survival.

What I do love are the family and friends who speak, because despite the sadness it's fascinating, enriching, to hear of a life distilled to its essence of goodness.

Rabbis often end a memorial service with 'may his memory be for a blessing' – that is, what lesson can we learn here? A man I was in love with: to live vividly and with passion. A school mum: the tonic of her joy. An old school mate: the gift of her friendship, the grace in her living. A near neighbour:

the shine of him near the end, as if his last years were spent in a perpetual state of chuckle.

So many aphorisms I've picked up during services and jotted on scrabbled tickets and receipts: Never suppress a kind thought. Be generous of spirit because it's bloody hard, for all of us. Pick up that phone. At the end of our lives the question should be not what we have done, but how well we have loved.

Lexi loved well. And like choirboys reaching a heartbreakingly higher purity just as their voices are about to break, she became piercingly perceptive towards the end, telling me what's what. 'I did it my way,' she sang, delighting in it. I wished I'd recorded her. Voice lodges longest in memory, can plunge us searingly back.

'People living deeply have no fear of death,' the author Anaïs Nin said. Lexi had no fear about living deeply, no fear about doing things her way. That was the lesson I learnt from a life driven by love and laughter; the sound of which I will carry forever in my head. She wasn't bound by what other people thought of her, right to the end – and with that, achieved an extraordinary lightness of being.

(Originally published in the *Weekend Australian Magazine*, 5 November 2011)

There's a place for us

Henry James called it 'a great good place' – a special place of calm and retreat that's just for you, no one else. A place where your eye rests. Where upon arrival you just ... breathe out. The prospect of it: a renovation of your serenity, a tonic. We all should have one. Do you?

It's often connected to childhood in some way. If not physically then in memory, a whiff of some happiness from long ago, like a Chinese whisper of solace. I think there's something spiritual in the urge to embrace some kind of homecoming as we age; the way we're drawn back to places where we began. The great circularity of life, perhaps, often acutely connected to landscape. 'We wove a web in childhood, a web of sunny air,' Charlotte Bronte wrote, and how beguiling that sounds, how understandable the want to recapture the sheer, unadulterated happiness of childhood; the very air of it, shift of its seasons, light. 'I love this town. I think sometimes of going into the ground here as a last wild gesture of love,' Marilynne Robinson wrote in one of my favourite novels, *Gilead*.

My great good places have always involved that quiet, humble, undervalued quality: simplicity. They're almost ridiculously anti-materialist. Shining hours in simple places; not much in the way of furniture or possessions; sometimes just a swag in a desert by a certain tree in a cherished riverbed, a secret place where the silence hums. With age I've needed the reparation of a great good place more and more; commensurate with a loss of materialism. Life is a process of simplification, isn't it? A stripping back.

The soldering principles of the great good place are leaking increasingly into the regular life. Right now, bound by the cram of kids, there's no time or means to seek one, to detach. So it has to be created around us. OK, that's a challenge. The office: a plywood plank resting across an armchair in the loungeroom. Six of us in three bedrooms, one bathroom, no bath – the baby's washed in the kitchen sink. But the happiness plumes through me in this lovely old teapot of a house, which rings with air and light and simplicity. Through wide windows the garden greenery tosses in the sea breeze like the heads of wild ponies; most of our London possessions are still in boxes, we're surviving with the bare minimum; but the joy to be had from just a trampoline, sprinkler and piece of soap! I'd dreamt of a place like this for so long in England, the homesickness increasingly corrosive over the years. But I can't say it's a break from the sheer intensity of motherhood.

I'm dreaming of a new great good place to escape to, now and then.

They always involve an immersion in nature. Being still and quiet with the land around us. We humans have such a vexed relationship with our planet, are like recalcitrant children with Mother Earth; fighting it, plundering, careless, unappreciative, rude. Australian writer Archie Weller said he could always sense the joy or sadness of places. Oh yes. For years, on and off, I lived in Sydney's Kings Cross and that was when a great good place was needed to flee to, desperately, because something feels so sad about that little city strip – someone said once it was the site of an Aboriginal massacre and goodness knows if it's true but it always struck me as a place crowded with lost, jittery, lonely ghosts.

Don't we all need to be closer to nature the closer we get to returning to it in death? When life is pummelling we need to seek out the solace of the land. Nature pressing close, feeling the great thumb of it, drawing strength from it. I hope you have a great good place to escape to, where at night you can feel as calm as an eiderdown lying snugly, quietly, in readiness on its bed. If not, seek one out.

(Originally published in the *Weekend Australian Magazine*, 12 November 2011)

A grand gesture

The elderly couple look like they're ready for the six o'clock Chinese meal at the RSL. They're dressed up and making the most of it. 'We love this place,' she declares with something akin to glee. 'We come here all the time,' he adds with pride.

They step from the James Bond-like pod that's plunged them deep into the cliff face and make their way towards an ethereal black Madonna floating like a Botticelli angel in a sea of gold, surrounded by butterflies that look like petals but hang on, come close – good grief – they're female bottoms, some spread in the glariest porn way. The couple take their time; there's a golden chair on a mountain lion rug facing the painting so they can gaze at the whole perplexing vision at their leisure. It's bizarre, cheeky, surreal. It's Hobart.

Welcome to the world of MONA, the most extraordinary museum I've ever seen. Our Bilbao. Destination travel in a way no other gallery in Australia can claim to be, and the international press is buzzing. It makes the dear, local institutions I've long cherished – the national and state galleries – seem positively cautious, tired. It's touched with genius and boldness and heart-soaring beauty. From the water droplets spelling out Google's top words like godly rain, to the cafe's blood-red macaroon on its black napkin and white plate, everything's been meticulously thought out. It's one man's eccentric, controlling, breathtaking vision.

He's David Walsh. Hobart born and bred, buck naked in the gallery catalogue, but that reduces the enigma he is. A mathematical genius who made his money from gambling, he could have bought 100 yachts and that would have been the boring end of him but he's done this, the most exhilarating act of public generosity I've ever seen here. Australia doesn't have a tradition of grand philanthropic gestures in the way the US does but my God, in the most transcendent, bar-setting way, he's showed up the rest of those who've made obscene wealth from our people and our land.

Mr Walsh, your country needs you. Your audacity. You lift the heart in terms of Aussies taking on the world. The visitors – many of them locals (it's free for them) – look as if they've had a shot of oxygen. It's fabulously invigorating in the way of all great art – bringing you closer to the wonder of what it is to be human in all its ugliness, of course, but in all its ravishing beauty, too. What we can create! MONA is the antithesis of a museum of hushed tones and fusty cabinets; it welcomes wonder. It outrages, seduces, moves, repels, but never, ever dulls. It's not deadened by the public purse, gets no government funding so hasn't had the energy sucked out of it by earnestness. It's taking on the world in the exhilarating way that the Opera House did, or *The Female Eunuch*, or a filmic reimagining of *Romeo and Juliet*. There's something so Australian about the vaulting audacity of our best creative spirits springing from seemingly nowhere; the no-holds barred ambition.

The building is carved deep into a sandstone cliff, the walls exposed, Jerusalem-like; they change, weep, blush with growth after strong rain. The glass floor of Walsh's apartment is the roof of a gallery corner; you may see him looking down at you roaming his wonderland, or catch his cat called Christ padding about the exhibits. His sister designed the funky staff jackets, his dad's ashes are displayed in an urn and I love those Rosebud touches of the personal that pulse through the place. Walsh is our enigmatic Citizen Kane who's given us something as intriguing and enduring as John Soane's Museum in London or the Frick in New York – one man's eccentric vision, built around the endearing domesticity of his own house. What a gift to the nation, but more importantly, what a gift to his home town. Lucky Hobart. Now can the rest of the country have a bit of you?

(Originally published in the *Weekend Australian Magazine*, 19 November 2011)

The slap

The shock of it was as viciously blunt as a slap across the face. Its haunting as potent as the cruellest of love affairs, whispering under my skin for years. The sheer bafflement of the whole thing. The silence that felled me. The friendship lost.

We'd met at baby group within the shock of first-time motherhood. Kindred spirits; exhausted, exhilarated; expats both in a foreign land. As more kids arrived we bestowed upon each other the gift of godparenthood, revelling in knowing we'd have each other for life. That sure. More open with each other than with either partner or parent. 'Grapple them to thy soul with hoops of steel,' Shakespeare wrote of friends, and I did.

Gradually our worlds widened beyond the gruelling intensity of early parenthood, those years when it felt like we were bunkering down and experimenting on our eldest, continually; trying to work out how to navigate the whole complex process. Confidence was gradually gained, routines crammed with new busy-ness. I went back to work, she didn't; kids went to different schools. I'd email to catch up – she was busy; soon, another time. In the few snatched coffees we managed I noticed a new snippiness from her about my life choices; an accumulation of pricks until my heart began to flinch in astonishment. Then ... nothing. Dropped into a cold, cold place. I heard her marriage was going through difficulties; I wrote, called, we'd shared everything once ... but she wouldn't let me in. 'I have lost friends, some by death ... others through sheer inability to cross the street,' Virginia Woolf wrote. This was loss through magnificent silence.

How to buckle a woman at the knees! It made me feel the one thing a friend should never make you feel – a failure – and I'd always tended my friendships like a gardener with a most cherished plot. Then an acquaintance, a fellow school mum, made me think about the cunning of withholding, its vicious ability to eat into another person. A woman whose every conversation was a form of competition, where there always had to be that moment of her triumph. I'd get a knot in my stomach when she called, felt sick when I saw her hovering at the school gate. I'd somehow allowed her into my life, through kids, yet she was one of those women I'd never have befriended pre-parenthood. It got to the point where she was vining my whole existence. But no, I could never fell her with silence – too unfeeling, cruel. I did, in the end, gently distance myself though. 'Friendships begin with liking or gratitude – roots that can be pulled up,' George Eliot said briskly.

So, what I've learnt over the years: that some friendships run their course and there's no shame in that. What seems nourishing at a certain time in your life may not be five years hence. As I get older, I need the soldering kind. That don't try to hurt or change the other person. Aren't judgmental. Involve a cherishing. That beautiful word, empathy. Are a balm amid the great wallop of life. And often it's not when times are bad you find out who your real friends are, but when times are good.

I have a friend – she won't mind me saying this – my best friend in primary and high school and best friend still. Now our children go to the same school and we sit in the playground at Friday pick-up, in one long golden stare at all the kids running about; yacking away then falling into silence. It's very hard to get up from that seat. Where we're both resting, for a moment, in the busy-ness of our days; in a great exhalation of stillness. Where we can just be ourselves, sitting side by side in the unspoken richness of the great arc of our lives. She's never judged, through all the ridiculous moments, never flattened. 'She gather me, man,' Toni Morrison wrote in her novel *Beloved*, 'the pieces I am, she gather them and give them back to me in all the right order.' Oh yes. With hoops of steel I hold her close.

(Originally published in the *Weekend Australian Magazine*, 26 November 2011)

Losing face

It's probably the angle. It couldn't be that bad. But there's a faint whiff of Bride of Wildenstein about it. A few more sessions with the needle and the look could harden, homogenise, and you'll start to look like all those other – insecure – women.

No Kylie, no, please not you. Please tell me it's just an unflattering shot, a trick of the light and the angle. But there's been feverish press speculation; you've admitted Botox usage in the past but not this time. I've always thought of you as impenetrable, magnificently, in terms of your media image. So tightly in control, spilling so little in interviews; the masterful game you've played. But perhaps with these latest pap shots we have a chink in the armour, and it's not revealing something good. It's revealing fear. Oh babes.

Our celeb-obsessed world greedily gulps up signs of slippage in a successful woman. We all stare, fascinated and appalled, at a beautiful face desecrated. But it makes me angry. At the men who impose their will upon it – because yes, it's usually men wielding the scalpel and needle – and angry at us for allowing it. I'm just as horrified seeing women tottering in those ridiculously vertiginous McQueen heels from a few years back, tumbling and falling on catwalks. Horrified to see Hussein Chalayan ugly-fying women in the name of fashion. Give me the female designers any day – Phoebe Philo, Marni's Consuelo Castiglioni, McQueen's successor, Sarah Burton, Jil Sander and our own Collette Dinnigan. They don't try to make us look ridiculous, don't try to stamp their misogyny upon us; they empower us with beauty and practicality and a flattering cut.

Would a female cosmetic practitioner see Kylie's famously pretty face, or Melanie Griffith's, or Meg Ryan's, and think, let me change this? Would they have the audacity? Can I apply my simple rule of equality here – are women doing this to men? There are some iconic females you never expect to succumb: Tilda Swinton. Cate Blanchett. Joan Didion. Julianne Moore. Quentin Bryce. Strong women all, with a compelling confidence. There's something comforting about finally owning your looks, accepting who you are; something courageous and cool about baring, honestly, the rich tapestry of your life through your face. I know a few older women with an intriguing serenity and strength, and they all have one thing in common: they're doing exactly what they want to be doing in life.

It's the serenity of being in control. The glow of it. And it comes from within.

The chap inquired not too long ago, 'Is that blue pen on your leg?' Er, no, that would be a varicose vein. He shrugged, didn't care. It's life. We're in it together and I love him for that shrug. Then there's the bosom – horrors! – turning into an old-lady shelf before my eyes, terrifyingly horizontal. But I'm comforted that the signs of slippage – thickening body, crepey upper lip, creased forehead – are something that mates are experiencing too. 'One of the signs of passing youth is the birth of a sense of fellowship with other human beings as we take our place among them,' Virginia Woolf wrote.

We don't get any sense of fellowship when we look at Melanie's face now, or Madonna's. It feels competitive, isolating, sad. That they're prisoners in their bodies, their esteem held hostage by the imperfections we all have as we age. It feels like the tipping point, when a celeb loses their currency. We want our older women to look strong and sexy and confident because they've got hard-earned wisdom and wit and wrinkles and a voice, finally. What younger women don't want blazing in an older woman's (unnaturally altered) face is fear.

A sheepdog willingness to please the blokes. Terror over ageing. Over death. Over the dewy-skinned young thing next to them. We're better than that, girls. It shouts to the world that you're scrabbling when you should be sailing in a sea of serenity and knowing. Kylie, you're not meant to be a scrabbler.

(Originally published in the *Weekend Australian Magazine*, 3 December 2011)

The last taboo

Is this the last frontier of sexual honesty? Is the lid being gently prised open on some kind of taboo here? Men who don't have sex. I know they're out there. But are they talking about it?

A woman I know hasn't slept with her long-term partner for six years. She's ready to explode. 'I feel like just walking into a pub and finding any bloke – I need sex.' She's in her late 30s, craving a child. Her man can't articulate why he has no sex drive. Refuses counselling. She wonders if he's gay. He's put on weight, and she suspects low self-esteem is a factor. 'I don't care if he's a bit chubbier. We've settled into this weird brother–sister relationship; it's just … killing me.' She loves him and can't bring herself to leave, despite the hunger for children. But rupture is so often good, I suggest. 'What happens if you're in your mid 40s and still with him and still not having sex? You'll be incredibly frustrated. And perhaps bitter.' She sighs, can't answer.

'I'm seeing more and more celibate relationships,' says Dr Lana Holstein, a sexuality expert. 'Typically, these are couples whose pace of life has increased so much that they're on the edge of exhaustion. That leaves little time for loving.' Stress, fatigue, performance anxiety are all culprits – not to mention the intensity of having young kids. 'Can you please write about lovemaking following childbirth,' pleaded a man in a heartbreaking letter. 'My wife and I couldn't recover from the loss of our sex life.'

Other men have given inklings of why sexual issues are so hard to discuss openly. One doesn't like fellatio but has never told his closest friends: 'To admit it would mean you're a nerd. It's like telling your mates you don't drive well or don't like footy.' Another wrote, 'I used to be embarrassed about hating this – then realised that a man who doesn't demand it comes as a great relief to women.' Others have boldly said they prefer something else to sex: 'It's the closeness and intimacy I really need, not the sex,' explained one. 'Just sleeping beside her is something I love,' emailed another. 'Being close, having her in my arms is such a joy.' 'Actually, I just want a cuddle a lot of the time.'

Then this: 'Dear Nikki, I'm 39 years old. I've been married for eight years, but with a difference. I'm a virgin, and so is my wife ... ' I thanked the correspondent for his courage in being so open, and wasn't sure I'd ever hear from him again. I did. 'The trouble is, my mother was the only woman I was ever comfortable with. My wife is the ideal woman in so far as she reminds me of my mum in terms of her qualities – but you don't sleep with your mum, do you? And Nikki, I'm shy, especially when it comes to the nitty-gritty. How does she put up with it? We have so much else in common, and we're both comfortable with the situation now.' My friend, whatever works. And it seems there's a lot of love in this relationship; love that's been soldered by a deep companionship and affection. As Margaret Atwood said, 'Nobody dies from lack of sex. It's lack of love we die from.'

Sex, of course, can be incredibly bleak, lonely, bewildering, ridiculous. But if it works ... well, there's nothing more life-affirming. There's something spiritual about the best sex; it's the most exhilarating mystery available to us. It can involve communicating with someone on the deepest, most profound level; revealing to them who we really are, surprising ourselves, and our partners, with the level of our surrender. Apart from the obvious biological imperative, good sex flushes us clean and boosts our confidence – and freshens and affirms a partnership. I'm haunted by that man's words, for they seem a logical extension of Joseph Conrad's infinitely sad aphorism: 'We live, as we dream – alone.' But sex, great sex, defies that. And of course from it comes that most wondrous decision in all of life: to create it.

(Originally published in the *Weekend Australian Magazine*, 10 December 2011)

A Christmas truce

He's gone. The headmaster of the boys' primary school. A country bloke. Finished up yesterday. The Education Department brought him out of retirement to turn a divided little school around. He did it, in a few short years. How? Civility. Chivalry. Courage. Such unfashionable words, eh?

Every afternoon this quiet, gentle man would stand at the gate farewelling his kids and seeing them safely across the road. It forced those children into meeting his eye, talking squarely to an adult, responding to the grace of his politeness. If they didn't then parents would nudge them to, drawn into the web of his decency. The school had been riven by a very contemporary, jittery frustration and was crying out for a balming.

Then recently, after a pick-up, the radio news had excerpts of Kyle Sandilands abusing a female journalist. From one world to another; it was like the car flinched, with grubbiness. My boys were riveted – and giggling, confused, at his use of the word 'titties'. Ah yes, this Australia, as opposed to that other, school-gate one. Kyle's repeat-offence verbal ugliness, Todd McKenney's vicious *Dancing with the Stars* attack on Lara Bingle, the battering ram of Tony Abbott's relentless negativity against Julia Gillard, Alan Jones wanting her tied up in a chaff bag and thrown out to sea, the 'Ditch the Witch' signs – the coarsening of public discourse. I don't want my three sons seeing these men as role models in terms of how to treat women, to learn from their tone. There's a lot of anger out there and it's directed at females who are doing things with their lives. Is there any correlation to the fact Australia has a healthy proportion of women in authority right now? It's exhilarating, on a world scale, yet the attacks speak of people threatened in the face of female empowerment.

This is written at the despairing behest of a male reader worried a particular brand of old-style Aussie chivalry seems to be leaching away like water into sand. The sweetness in the smile of the late John Hargreaves encapsulated it. Older men seem to embody it most. The retiring principal, perhaps your grandfather, the bloke under my 98-year-old grandmother's first-floor flat. Nan lives alone and is helped along by Max, who cleans the cobwebs off her windows with an old pair of undies attached to his fishing rod and they all have a laugh but the main thing is, he's watching over her. It's chivalrous, courteous, kind, in a hysterically funny Aussie way.

As parents we're teaching our children to wake up to the wonder of this world and its beauty. Children watch us. And do as we do. Especially at Christmas, when so many of us have the pressure cooker of family around us. For 15 years I've been dreaming of an Aussie Christmas, of uncurling the frozen bones under the Southern light, waking to a cram of birds and a sliver of hard sun through the curtains. Dreaming of a morning dip at the beach, telling the kids to skedaddle and get the cricket match going, then the late afternoon kip under a tin roof, creaking in the heat, that's soon to be danced on by possums ...

I'm about to get the dream in a country that should be counting its blessings in terms of buoyancy – believe me, they've really got something to whinge about in Europe. The world undergoes a surge of meaning at this time, a little ocean swell of loveliness, and my wish is a Christmas truce in all the negativity, a pause where we can be a little kinder, courteous, to each other. I've been to several carol singalongs recently and something keeps catching at my heart: the way we slip into living within the world, rather than alongside it, as we age. Kyle exists alongside rather than within it, unlike the cherished man just retired from his happy little school. These holidays I wish Kyle the solace of love, and serenity, and belonging – and a generous heart. I wish everyone these things, in abundance.

(Originally published in the *Weekend Australian Magazine*, 17 December 2011)

Eyes wired open

I have a fractious relationship with the dark hours; we fall in and out of love.

Once, pre children, I loved the velvety quiet of night time, when I'd gallop the writing surrounded by a slumbering neighbourhood, fuelled by chocolate and champagne. Neurophysiologically, we have a creativity and an energy peak between two and four in the mornings. Sylvia Plath wrote in the early hours before her kids were awake. Her writing has that sharpness and tautness and hysteria of 4am; and look what happened to her.

As for me, now, cripes – harangued by wakefulness at 3am. The baby is finally sleeping overnight yet I'm haunted, still, by the imprint of his feeding times. With frustrating regularity my mind jolts from slumber like a steel trap sprung open. Thoughts are freed, pinging and zipping. Writing lines to be jotted down; emails checked from my old world, London; battle plans drawn up to tackle the child-crammed day ahead;

ridiculously small worries that torment with sudden, obscene wilfulness – only to fade into insignificance in the light of a new day. The result: a life, right now, held hostage by sleep. The lack of it, the craving for it, the conspiring to get it. It feels like a very modern scourge, this inability to switch off.

US blogger Arianna Huffington passed out from exhaustion, broke her cheekbone and got five stitches over her eye. Since then she's declared lack of sleep 'a feminist issue' and wants women to achieve at least seven straight hours of slumber a night. I wish …

Girlfriends talk about a lie-in with a passion and urgency that's absent from talk about sex; we dream of Shakespeare's 'sleep that knits up the ravell'd sleeve of care'. We're in love with it: wondering why we can't get enough of it, feeling guilty when we do. Feminism's given us the right to expect relationships, career and children all at once but it's also given us a new level of exhaustion. One girlfriend told me her husband had fallen asleep inside her while making love. 'He was exhausted from work – and I was relieved, because I was exhausted, too. I just rolled him off and went to sleep. It's all we want now.'

I know a high-powered career woman who existed on four hours a night. She could never sleep with a man beside her; because of the trust in it, the relaxing. She was very tight and controlled, had never had an orgasm, had never worked out how to let go; she'd surrounded herself with a boundary of no.

At 38 she fell in love with a man who slept with the abandon of a child, limbs splayed. He taught her to relax. Gave her her first orgasm. And for the first time in her life she slept soundly by the side of a man and discovered the sweetness of an arm winging her torso in slumber, the arch of his foot locked into her calf, and waking together into the cleanness of a new day.

I find shared sleep deeply sexy; often more so than making love. It's where true love lies, beyond words, beyond sex. 'Love does not make itself felt in the desire for copulation (a desire that extends to an infinite number of women) but in the desire for shared sleep (a desire limited to one woman),' the Czech author Milan Kundera wrote in *The Unbearable Lightness of Being*.

The problem for the chap and I is that with all our young kids it's a constant round of musical beds in our house, so the two of us rarely end up in the same bed. We can't wait to climb beyond these fractured early years of parenting. Saying that, few things are sweeter than a child falling into the heaviness of slumber in your arms. At night I breathe in deep their sleeping, my heart welling with love – and envy. Oh for the vastness of that safe, secure, replenishing oblivion. I yearn for the gift of it, unbroken, for 12 hours straight. 'Balm of hurt minds ... chief nourisher in life's feast.' Shakespeare, again, of course.

(Originally published in the *Weekend Australian Magazine*, 21 January 2012)

ABC of equality in education

'Having your prospects determined at birth is the most pernicious and fundamental form of inequality.'

That damning judgment was copied into my journal several years ago as a blazing reminder why I needed to find my way home. It was *The Spectator* magazine's grim conclusion in terms of education in Britain. The politics of envy has sourly infected that land, and nowhere is it more apparent than the teaching of young people. Despair was all around us, from parents who knew that a first-class education is the greatest gift they can give their kids – and more often than not in this new England they'd have to pay for it. Hugely. And many, simply, couldn't. Broken Britain indeed.

The ugly truth dawned at preschool level over there: that richer, thicker kids would end up getting further ahead than poorer, brighter kids. Whether we could afford private education or not I didn't want my children growing up in that world; I wanted the bracing rigour of a meritocracy.

Our local, hugely expensive nursery in London was a feeder school for Prince William's old pre-prep, itself a conveyer belt into feeders for the likes of Eton and Westminster, which of course are well-worn paths to Oxbridge. So. The shaping of the British elite – and by the same measure, its underclass – begins at three, and with the demise of the UK's selective, government-funded grammar schools from the '60s onwards it wasn't looking good for children without access to that golden path. UK politicians come from an increasingly narrow pool – the PM, his deputy and chancellor all went to schools with fees higher than the average wage; they're all Oxbridge graduates, as is the Leader of the Opposition. And they wonder why there were riots.

Then we arrived in Oz. Before the car situation was worked out we were using cabs a lot. One thing the drivers said again and again – whether from Afghanistan or Albania or Algeria – was that you could be anything in Australia, do anything, if you worked hard enough. And for a lot of them that was a beacon, not so much for themselves but for their children. It's the great Australian dream, and as someone newly arrived in the land it felt exhilarating. Felt like the future. Intensely exciting for my children to be a part of. As a British friend residing in Australia said, 'Here, no one can box you into a corner unless you want to be boxed into a corner. That's just not the case in the UK.'

We came from a Britain where more than a million young people are unemployed. As I farewelled a cherished educator he said, 'You're doing the right thing. The future is China and Southeast Asia. There'll be so many opportunities for your kids as they grow up.'

Britain's coalition government is admirably trying to turn the stricken ship around, helmed by its reformist education minister Michael Gove. He's cleared the path for 'free schools', government-funded but often parent- or teacher-led, removed from the stifling control of local councils. Writer Toby Young set up one. His moving aim: 'To take a black kid from a local housing estate, feed him on a diet of Plato, Aristotle, Hobbes, Locke, Austen and Dickens, get him into Oxford and then sit back and watch as he goes on to become Prime Minister.'

Meanwhile in Australia, there's the robust tradition of state selectives. According to one survey, NSW's top 10 schools in 2011, in terms of HSC results, were all state selectives except for one. Imagine them being shut down as ostentatiously divisive? That's what a British Labour government decided in the '60s, and the Tories never reversed that decision. The consequences are there to see now. My kids were a part of that world and, frankly, I'm so grateful we're here. A country where a fair whack of its top schools are state? As a nation, that's something to be proud of.

(Originally published in the *Weekend Australian Magazine*, 28 January 2012)

A car is a woman's shed

The scene: the local pool with a bunch of school mums, my four-year-old gently strumming her fingers through my hair.

I'm yakking on about how I sometimes get so tired after school runs or grocery shops that I just sit in the car outside the house afterwards, immobile, for five or 10 minutes, in the lovely cosy silence that doesn't talk back at me; in one huge and restoring exhalation of stillness. These 'car moments' are just as therapeutic as a bloke's shed, and we women agree we all need them in our lives. We sink into companionable silence contemplating that heavenly little pocket of peace in the great cram of our days; mine made lovely by the fingers sifting through my hair like a tiny, tender rake.

As if on cue, the fingers' owner pipes up: 'I think you've got nits, Mummy.' Oh for the soothing balm of a private car moment that instant! Alas, no escape. Everyone is laughing, and looking slightly aghast, and inching away as once again it is confirmed to me: I am the woman who makes other mothers feel good about themselves. And who craves at that very moment the privacy and peace, restoration and escape of her shed on wheels.

The wonders of a car for a woman! Not just when stationary post-supermarket but on the road, of course, as well. How I love those times when I can revel in my playlist without anyone groaning, sing very loudly, chuckle with the lovely gentleman on the radio and generally let the mind run amok with a richness of thinking that's hard to get within the great roar of home life; oh yes, there I am in my car, as happy as a goat in a garden.

Occasionally the dear and perceptive chap, in an effort to preserve the sanity of his marriage, senses that something is at breaking point. 'Just go,' he commands.

No encouragement is needed. I skedaddle. Favourite moments? Gunning alone along country roads, windows down, music up, elbow resting on the door, sun and wind-whipped; my hand reaching up to butt the breeze. The writer in me uncurling – no distraction, no depletion, no rubbing out. 'Driving is a spectacular form of amnesia,' the French philosopher Jean Baudrillard declared. 'Everything is to be discovered, everything to be obliterated.' Oh yes. As a woman, it's the one empowering place you're in control. Motherhood is about the loss of control, a loosening, letting go; and that can be swamping.

Then there's Saudi Arabia, where women can be arrested if they get behind the wheel. Repeated campaigns have tried to get the religious edict overturned; Amnesty International says the authorities 'must stop treating women as second-class citizens' because the ban is 'an immense barrier to their freedom of movement'. It reminds me of a line by the male protagonist, Newland Archer, in Edith Wharton's *The Age of Innocence*. '"Women ought to be free – as free as we are," he declared, making a discovery of which he was too irritated to measure the terrific consequences.'

Postscript: the car moment following the swimming pool incident? Contemplating the grim fact that, as the mother of four including a baby, nits will feature in my life for the next, oh, 15 years. Right. Can I just say I used the nit comb vigorously that night, as I do after every hair wash. Clear.

I had a little word to my daughter. She looked at me sceptically. I was heading off on an extremely rare night out after the latest birth. Her father said, to break the impasse, 'Doesn't Mummy look beautiful?' 'Not yet,' she replied in that brutally honest way of a four-year-old. We have a long way to go.

But one thing I do know is that I'll never stop her driving. Because, as her parent, I'll always want her soul to sing.

(Originally published in the *Weekend Australian Magazine*, 4 February 2012)

Creatively confined

'Daddy's spending his birthday in jail,' the four-year-old's declaring to all and sundry as I run around hosing spot fires of speculation.

In everyone's faces: the aghast speculation, the struggle with politeness. She's absolutely right – we're in jail. Not just the chap but all of us. Newcastle's old colonial lock-up, complete with iron padlocks and padded cells and a graffitied exercise yard with its grim outdoor bath. I've been offered a writer's residency in what's now a cultural centre and the tribe's tagging along for the experience. I struggle to type. If anyone gets any louder I'm locking up the lot of them and throwing away the key. Doh! Screams of exhilaration. You see, as a kid it's wildly exciting having the run of this place. We're all alone at night and are eager for some kind of paranormal experience but honestly, I think we've frightened away the resident ghost. Poor thing. We're that loud, there are lots of stone walls to echo off – and central Newcastle's awfully quiet.

Driving down the main drag on Sunday afternoon is like cruising along an abandoned film back lot; a scene from *On The Beach* as life leaks away from all populated areas. Don't get me wrong, Newcastle's booming, just not in its once-very-beautiful heart. It's enough to make the town burghers of its robust past weep. David Jones' windows are now blacked out and scrappy-dusty in their prized mall location. NSW's oldest theatre, the Victoria, is boarded up, the grand old dame just waiting for an ungagging, all her glory intact from fly tower to circle foyer. The magnificent wedding cake of a post office with its honeyed sandstone is insulted by hoardings and a wire fence topped by barbed wire. A lone white digger stands out the front, head bowed in solemnity and grief, as if contemplating an Australia lost. All the beautiful buildings, wilting and abandoned like so many Miss Havershams lost in their ghostly memories. The CBD feels like it's winding down, heartbreakingly, right under the council's nose.

The one beautifully maintained heritage building? The Town Hall, of course, that's overlooked a decade of depletion in this once proud hub of the mighty Hunter. The only people who seem to have any energy and dynamism amid the CBD's astonishing ennui are the camera-wielding parking inspectors, puffed with entitlement and the thrill of the kill. And that's part of the problem. There's three hours free parking at the Westfield 10 minutes' drive from here, but a world away in terms of bustling crowds. You can also get free parking at the very cool Darby Street precinct, the creative hub of the region. While in town I spend a lot of frustrating time hopping from CBD meter to meter (challenging with a baby in tow) and often the machines mysteriously don't want to read my card. I give up and head to Westfield. It's easier, and free.

But all is not lost. A dynamic little initiative called 'Renew Newcastle' is fighting back, fuelled by a tide of Novocastrians aghast at what's happening as big businesses, health providers and major retailers abandon ship to outlying areas. The aim: to refuse to let a cherished CBD die around it. How? By encouraging artists and visionaries to revitalise empty retail spaces with pop-up shops, design collectives and galleries, drawing in people with quirkiness and originality and beauty. It feels like the cool people are taking over. The organisation's Marni Jackson says, 'There've always been interesting things going on here, but we've brought them to the fore.' Their passionate model for renewal is now being replicated in waning areas of Adelaide, Geelong, Townsville and Lismore.

Newcastle's CBD needs all the help it can get. I want it to be – as they say in these parts – as full as the last bus out of BHP on a Friday night. Let's start with an art gallery or library in the post office, right next to the ingeniously revived Lock-up Cultural Centre. A new creative precinct for a very cool, arty city? Fabulous.

(Originally published in the *Weekend Australian Magazine*, 11 February 2012)

Death of a romantic

In my early 20s I lived in a share house – with one particular flatmate I barely knew.

He was younger than the rest of us, a student, quiet, and he never really participated in the rambunctious life of the house. Our gentle tenant had just broken up, traumatically, with a woman a decade older. He was still in love, his life held hostage by his obsession. He stayed mostly in his room. The rest of us got on with our lives; we were starting careers, and work consumed us in that self-obsessed 20-something way.

On the first day of spring, a Saturday, my flatmate suggested I come for a drive. He cruised around his childhood haunts – home, primary and high schools, corner shop. He was chatty and buoyant, it was a lovely afternoon; perhaps things were looking up. When we returned he went to his room as he always did. That evening he left for another drive.

The police knocked on our door several hours later. He had hanged himself in the grounds of his girlfriend's house.

The shock, the anguish, the guilt, and over the months I interrogated the scraps of time I'd spent with him – did I do enough? Could I have stopped him? Helped? For someone who touched my life so lightly he became suddenly huge in it, and has haunted it ever since.

On his bed he'd left a careful tableau of childhood photos, sports certificates and school reports, with a note at its centre:

'I love _____ forever.'

I can still recall his handwriting. It was like a child's. The jolt of that. When his father came around – pale with bewilderment, barely able to speak – I saw he knew very little about his only son, whose face was like a Chinese whisper of his. He was desperate to understand. None of us in the house was really able to help.

Why did my flatmate do it? Obsession, infatuation, the fire and volatility of youth. He was bound by desire in a consumingly negative way – and in failed love can lie the weeds of mad actions and destruction. Oh, I've been there. Felled by passion, a despairing member of that exclusive club, heartbreak.

It took my parents and friends a long while – three years – to haul me back into optimism. I'm much more practical about romantic love now; no longer an avid fan. It's such a transient, delusional, debilitating concept. It can take possession of your life, and your senses. But usually only once. Relationships following the Big One are often shrewder, calmer, more realistic – and more healthy because of that.

The archetypal lovers who embodied the passion I once aspired to were Heathcliff and Cathy. In a scene in *Wuthering Heights* where Heathcliff lets go of the love of his life, Emily Bronte writes that there were 'four distinct impressions left, blue in the colourless skin'. That sounds painful, and in these relationships there's often a lot of pain.

'This last night we tear into each other, as if to wound, as if to find the key to everything before morning,' Michael Ondaatje wrote in *Coming Through Slaughter*, the book I always carry with me as a tuning fork for my own fiction. But it's not a restful, replenishing relationship he's writing about. Passion craves quietness, security, calm – states hard to attain in romantic love. And sometimes, as the worm turns, hurting is a way of holding someone. Above all I felt unanchored during my youthful infatuation, and a rich, mature, requited love should feel like a harbour, a haven, to rest from all the toss of the world.

It took many years of living to realise that.

Why am I still so haunted by my flatmate? Because I just wish that beautiful boy, so bursting with potential, had grown up and known other women – had journeyed to a point where he could look back and laugh. I wonder, all these years later, that if he could reflect he'd be thinking, 'Damn it, why did I do it? For her?' I suspect he would. And it breaks my heart, still.

(Originally published in the *Weekend Australian Magazine*, 18 February 2012)

Why be a writer?

'Waste of time, that,' gruffed my father when first told of the writing dream many, many years ago.

It almost stopped me in my tracks; I was that much of a yes-girl, pleasing programmed into my female DNA. I tumbled into radio journalism, used that as a front for the secret passion; Dad had no idea. He was happy, I was happy. But the want was too insistent, and alongside the reporter's notebook was always the writer's journal. Jotting, endlessly jotting, conversation scraps, title ideas, the taste of a sky, the sadness of a smile, the whisper of a story.

Six novels down the track I'm asked again and again by aspiring writers how on Earth it's done; what's the secret. God knows, I'm always thinking, it doesn't get any easier. Write as if you're dying, I tell them; it's a great motivator. It's a little like Liza Minnelli's advice to an aspiring singer: 'Remember to sing every song as if it's the last time you are ever going to sing it.'

That secret formula? Tenacity. Discipline. Self-belief. The ability to keep at it no matter how many heart-sinkers there are around you; all those people telling you to give up, all those swamping rejection slips and, believe me, I've had a few. The apprenticeship was short stories, for years, sent off in scatter bombardment to Australia's various literary journals and gradually I'd find that someone, somewhere, would gloriously, soaringly, take one. An early heart-lifter? Les Murray, *Quadrant* magazine's literary editor, who sent me a rocket-booster of confidence when he accepted a story about three generations of coal miners in the family. Dad didn't read it. I didn't show him. Wouldn't dare.

It's never been easy, the writer's journey. Bank managers always look at me askance when the chap and I try to get a mortgage ('I think we'll just stick with your husband's details'). The mentor was the wise and gentle novelist Glenda Adams, during an MA in Creative Writing. 'Nikki, the hardest thing is to get the reader to keep turning the page, to not bore them.' By oath, and I've had her words in my head ever since. Always close by, a postcard of a Picasso bather – for its sheer audacity and energy. That's not a bather but it is, of course. And the Ezra Pound battle cry: 'Make it new.' It's the aim, as a novelist. Create something fresh and startling and bold, a new voice, a new way. Risk. Dare. Disturb. 'For a true writer each book should be a new beginning where he tries again for something that is beyond attainment,' Ernest Hemingway said in his Nobel acceptance speech, 'he should always try for something that has never been done or that others have tried and failed.' And never forget the need to enchant. Draw a curtain around the reader; cosy them in. 'A book ... needs something to say and it needs to know how to say it,' the British editor Simon Prosser said. 'As readers, we want to be flirted with, flattered, gripped, excited, seduced, transported. (It's hard to avoid the language of the erotic.)'

What I've learnt over the years: writing hurts. Women who write feel too much. Honesty is the most potent thing of all – it's amazing how much support you get when you tell the truth. And it's the hardest thing I'll ever do but nothing else gives me such a quietness of the soul; I'll not be talked out of it.

My beloved Dad didn't impart any writing skills. But he gave me a sense of persistence, and tenacity. He first went down the pit at 16 – and after a lifetime of all manner of jobs he's underground again (born 1934, that's the Aussie mining boom for you). When he settles down with a tome now he hates the light from those newfangled bulbs, so puts on his old miner's cap lamp to read. It's never my books. My first novel, *Shiver*, had a word on page one he didn't like. He snapped it shut and hasn't read a single one since. I'm, er, rather pleased about that.

(Originally published in the *Weekend Australian Magazine*, 25 February 2012)

Impure thoughts

The letter was responding to a recent column about men who don't have sex, detailing a stressful love life with his ex, failure to perform because of anxiety – but then it went off piste.

'There's another factor that dare not raise its head. A taboo topic never discussed except in the quiet company of drunk men. An issue that's a gigantic obstacle for men … cleanliness. I'm the first to admit that males aren't a bastion of light when it comes to it, but here's the struggle. Nothing evaporated sexual desire quicker, (yet) how to raise it without the poor girl feeling like a complete disgrace? To this day I haven't told her. She'd be distraught with shame. There are millions of us guys who experience the "thriller killer" but say nothing.'

Intriguing – yet my correspondent's aversion has the weight of thousands of years of religious doctrine behind him; across many cultures is embedded a contempt for women's bodies and their natural functions, in practice and text. The Bible states a woman is unclean during her period; if she gives birth to a girl she'll be unclean for twice as long as she will be if she has a son. During the beautiful Christmas hymn 'O Come All Ye Faithful' is the bizarre bombshell, 'Lo! He abhors not the virgin's womb.' Er, why should he? In Islam, a woman's not allowed to offer prayer or fast or circumambulate Mecca's Kaaba during her menses, and sexual intercourse is prohibited. In the Hindu faith, women are prevented from participating in normal life while menstruating; they must be 'purified' before returning to their family.

And veering from all that is the recent ordeal of eight-year-old Naama Margolese, harassed in Israel by ultra-Orthodox extremists while walking to her religious Jewish girls' school. Black-hatted men spat on her and called her a whore for dressing 'immodestly' – she was wearing long sleeves and a below-the-knee skirt but it wasn't enough. 'When I walk to school … I used to get a tummy ache because I was so scared … that they were going to stand and start yelling and spitting,' she said. 'They don't want us to go to the school.' Ah yes, could that be because they don't want women empowered by education; don't want them unleashed, with a potent voice? Thus the roar of men's anger across the millennia; the roar of them trying to clamp women down. What are they afraid of?

And so those male-saturated religions deem us unclean, lesser. Convenient. And of course never do we feel more empowered, exhilarated and in control than when we're doing the one thing men can't: give birth.

A mucky, earthy process. I defecated during labour – something the female body can instinctively do. I'm not proud of it but not ashamed, either. I don't consider it unclean; I am not revolted, although I'm sure my letter-writer is. I surrendered to the animal within. Gave birth on all fours. It felt instinctively right. Didn't adopt the lithotomy position, where the mother lies on her back with her feet in stirrups. Some say it was developed by doctors in France at the command of Louis XIV, who wanted to watch a mistress give birth. Thanks guys. No position could be worse for a woman in labour because she's working uphill, against gravity, to expel the baby – and she's not in control.

My middle-aged guilty-as-porn delight of the moment: YouTubing Madonna rocking the recent Super Bowl. Deliciously camp, soaringly beautiful, cheeky. Men as her slaves in that temple of all things alpha male, their torsos rippling in servitude as they wheel in Her Golden-ness. She's 53, a mum, and loving it. She plastered that blokey, hetero holy ground with moving *Vogue* covers and captivated the world. Less than a week later there were Adele, Alicia Keys, Taylor Swift and Jennifer Hudson singing their hearts out at the Grammys, the men around them seeming curiously underpowered, old, tired in comparison. It felt like the future, boys. Whether you like it or not.

(Originally published in the *Weekend Australian Magazine*, 3 March 2012)

Regrets? Here are a few

I wish I'd had the courage to live a life true to myself – not the life others expected of me. It's the number one regret of the dying, in all their crystal-clear lucidity.

In her book *The Top Five Regrets of the Dying*, Bronnie Ware, who worked for years as a palliative carer, has published the five regrets she heard again and again. So herewith notes to self, starting with that number one: don't be bound by fear of failure. Think of all those hesitations to leap into something risky because of fear – yet the only true failing, of course, is in not doing anything. We need to appreciate setbacks; acknowledge the courage it's taken to get that far. Try saying a little more 'I will' rather than 'I should'. Appreciate change. Rupture's a gift, always, in some way. Our lives are made rich by risking, not by surrounding ourselves with a boundary of 'no'. And to live that life true to yourself you have to stop worrying about what other people think of you. 'Arm me, audacity,' Shakespeare said. Yes.

Number two regret: I wish I hadn't worked so hard. This from people horrified that so much of their lives was spent on the great treadmill of just getting by. Our ambitions so often, of course, involve that voracious god of Mammon. But a life driven by love is preferable to a life driven by greed; the Gina Rinehart saga teaches us that happiness has nothing to do with obscene accumulations of unshared wealth. It lies in the simplest of moments. Walking down to the sea. Impromptu sunset barbies with mates. My mother brushing my daughter's hair. A song irrepressibly launching me into dancing (sorry kids, I know this one's excruciating for you). Hearing the bell at my boys' school, from home, as I write; calling them out to play as I keep tabs on the happy rhythm of their day. The Aussie bush in the golden hour of sunset when everything stills, pauses, softens. So. Exhale. Stop. Never forget the potency of silence, and simplicity. My guide in all this, Emily Dickinson, seizing the wonder in living: 'Friday I tasted life. It was a vast morsel. A Circus passed my house. Still I feel the red in my mind ... The lawn is full of south and the odours tangle, and I hear to-day for the first time the river in the tree.'

Regret number three: I wish I'd had the courage to express my feelings. Sartre said an essential freedom is the ability to say no. But do we do it, enough? It's strong people who have the courage to show their vulnerability. The constant constraint of the pleaser, the yes person, can be incredibly depleting. Women, especially, fall into this trap. Feelings aren't honestly articulated, and what can result is a festering resentment, a corrosive bitterness – I've noticed this particularly with some women of the pre-feminist generation. They weren't meant to shout loud, weren't taught to, and the frustration eats through them.

Number four: I wish I'd stayed in touch with friends. Life closes over us, we lose contact with people, drift away – but as my beloved Aunty Kay says, there's not a person alive who doesn't want to be told they're loved. There are three cherished people I've let drift, ridiculously, in the great rush of life. This will be rectified. And of course, doing something for someone else helps not only them, but ourselves; it buoys us.

So to number five, the most poignant of the lot: I wish I'd let myself be happier. Such a simple thing. Years ago I was living in a shared house in Alice with a succession of gorgeous women, all working hard, cooking up a storm, playing, loving, laughing a lot. 'Never lose your sense of ludic, girls!' declared a visiting artist. But we do, as worries and responsibilities gather pace. Yet the bad times dissolve, always. The lows come into our lives to draw us into the vast, glittery vividness of what it is to be human, so we can then venture into the world wiser, richer, more compassionate. And a sense of ludic, a light heart? It's a great armoury for living. The dying teach us that.

(Originally published in the *Weekend Australian Magazine*, 10 March 2012)

Parenting? Let's be honest ...

I'd volunteered for the cupcake stall at the school fair. 'Making or selling?' enquired the mum at the gate.

'Selling.'

'Thank God,' her relief almost cartoon-enormous.

Everyone's laughing at the one who's the benchmark of non-domestica. But do you really want to be known for your baking prowess? I'm with Carrie Bradshaw: the oven's used for storage, and five of our kitchen cupboards are crammed with books.

God help the kids. 'Whatever works' is the philosophy. Parenting is a process of letting go; relinquishing control of that tight little existence you were once so firmly in command of.

Yes, the baby's still breastfed, but there are no qualms about a hearty dose of formula. 'He's having his McDonald's!' yells the chap to neighbours when he's out wheeling wee Jago, bottle in mouth. Yes, my kids eat sweets, but the standard was set a generation ago: Milo on white bread sandwiches every day of school life. How on Earth am I still alive? Yes, my kids watch TV and sometimes it's even used for babysitting to, er, finish a column – but I do recall growing up watching *The Brady Bunch, Hogan's Heroes, Gilligan's Island* and *Green Acres* for hours on end, every afternoon – as did every kid around me. How can we function in this world? Where were the parents? Not hovering like they do now, that's for sure. A mate earned his way through uni by being paid to watch *Days of Our Lives* each day and deliver a detailed summary. The employer? His working mum. How times have changed.

What I'd love is a bit more honesty in the parenting world, because it's bloody hard, for all of us. It can be such a haranguing, judgmental little battlefield. Can't we just value each other? We all have our short cuts, guilty secrets. Mine? That sometimes it's cereal for dinner. Scrambled eggs, too often, because it's easy and doesn't involve flour. That I've been known to eat an entire packet of chocolate biscuits furtively behind a cupboard like a grubby thief, the kids oblivious by the telly. That my life's been so overtaken by everyone's black socks that I've given up ever sorting them; they're in a basket now, to be delved into by everyone but me. That I turn into someone else when tired; a voice snaps out in a tone of anger and ugliness that I'm ashamed of, yet still it roars. Dirty T-shirts? Sometimes flipped inside out. My kids have never had a home-made birthday cake and, yes, I've smacked. How have any of them survived?

No help either, apart from a cleaner. There were afternoon nannies in London, but I found it deadens the relationship between you and your kids. Yes, it's more even, but there are less of the vivid lows and crucially, the soaring highs. The Aussie childminders around me – earning bucketloads as the most-coveted nationality in the nannying stakes – would tell me repeatedly they'd never raise their own kids this way. Telling. Because you need to muck in with them, get your hands dirty; don't want that distance between you like a glass wall in a bank. Or do you? Being a parent puts you at the coalface of living in all its wretched exhaustion and competitiveness and depletion and ugliness – but in all its incandescence, too.

So now we're muddling through with my pathetic attempts at cooking. Miss Four, who has just learnt the art of the compliment, said proudly recently: 'This is the first meal I've ever liked, Mummy!' (Chicken and broccoli curry in satay sauce – as complex as it'll ever get.)

Then there's the poor, dear chap. During my flying trip to England last year, my sister's mate was roped in to look after the family. And, er, cooked. For weeks afterwards there were late-night laments emanating from the kitchen: 'I married the wrong one.' They'll start up again when the chap reads these words and all the slings and arrows of outrageous fortune are freshened up for him once again. Non-domestic-type recipes and secret-embarrassment-as-parent stories are always most welcome in this land. I can't be the only one, surely?

(Originally published in the *Weekend Australian Magazine*, 17 March 2012)

Straight from the heart

A handwritten letter arrived yesterday. It felt like a celebration of stillness. It's been some time since anyone close had sat down and written, pen in hand, at length to me.

It was a little depth charge from the past; reminded me of John Donne's lovely words, 'letters mingle souls'.

It was sent from England, on a whim, by a friend filling up a quiet morning in a country kitchen anointed by the first sun of spring; that shy little flower, the snowdrop, making its first appearance outside, along with two swans on a tributary of the Avon that her medieval mill-house nudges up against. She described the world around her so vividly, a landscape cracking open after the bitterness of winter. There were no crossings-out, it was considered yet spontaneous, a lovely combination. I could almost feel the imprint of her worn kitchen table that she wrote at, that I've sat at many times over the years, yakking away, and now miss very much. Then there was the paper; the heaviness of it, creaminess, sensuality.

It was the antithesis of a recent dinner party. 'Google me,' said the stranger beside me, spelling out the intricacies of her name instead of just telling me a little something of herself. I left early. I had googling to do. Ah, modern life. I like observing people, slowly; a Google persona tells me little and can give the wrong impression entirely; whereas a heartfelt letter can feel like a baring of the soul. And why on Earth would anyone want Google to be the shopfront to the person they are? It reminded me that the older I get the less I want to meet new people; I spend scarcely enough time with cherished friends and have little time now for the clutter of anyone else.

I wrote back to my friend, not wanting to drop the ball that had been tossed. Carved out a slice of stillness in a busy day, forcing myself into a soul-concentration as her reverie was answered with another. The words came strong. It felt good, replenishing; felt like a turning towards authenticity. And this from someone whose main mode of communication now is email. But they so often feel dashed, harried; misspellings and carelessness diminishing them. Rarely do they feel like a connection of the soul. I think of the potency of letters past, from decades ago: my grandmother's, barely a full stop in them, the hand spidery but the voice strong. Love letters that addled me, break-up letters scanned with a thumping heart, letters brimming with Hermann Hesse quotes from backpacking mates. Each one in a hand as memorable as voice; some as sharp and as shocking as a slap. So many kept:

a greeting on the back of a test, a ripped-out journal page, a careful phrase on a gum leaf. And then from about a decade ago, a vast dropping off. A great gulf of silence and a volume of emails I'll never bother printing out. The handwritten letter is not just about communication, but communion – that spiritually softened word of connection and grace.

Writing shelters me. My own, as I do it; but also other people's. And this letter sheltered me for a blessed moment of stillness. How do you write stillness? I've always wondered if it was possible, and my friend came close. I didn't rip open her envelope at once but waited for quietness; made a cup of tea, readied myself. There was something of a ritual to it. It was the shining time as I read the tonic of her words. As Goethe said, 'we lay aside letters never to read them again, and at last we destroy them out of discretion, and so disappears the most beautiful, the most immediate breath of life …' Oh yes. In this world of homogenisation, of all the clattery chattery declarations and posturings of Facebook and Twitter, I appreciate 'other'. Want to be 'other', seek it out. This letter, vividly, was 'other'. Quietly, beautifully. I wonder if it'll be the last ever received from a cherished friend. I hope not.

(Originally published in the *Weekend Australian Magazine*, 24 March 2012)

The real Julia fan club

It felt something like blasphemy.

A declaration as risky, difficult and defining as an admission to church-going, or loving a book you wouldn't be caught dead reading on a train but have secretly downloaded on your e-reader. Just three simple words, setting off a little explosion of shock within the collected school-gate psyche. 'I adore Julia.' Dead silence. The perpetrator added, emboldened, 'I'm coming out.' Another mum piped up, 'I adore her, too.' They looked at each other, amazed; it was like stumbling across some secret society of disparate females expressing deeply unfashionable, unspoken sentiments. Why? I ventured. 'Because if I had a dinner party she'd be the one who'd stay back and help me do the dishes at the end.' Unlocked, the mum added, 'We're all scared of saying we love her – in front of men, especially. It's like saying you're a feminist.'

Among certain women there's a jarring disconnect between what they're thinking and the narrative they're being fed that is 'Julia'. What they see: a woman getting things done. In a man's world. Quietly, differently, effectively. Amid the great roar of vitriol, and not flinching. They think it's extraordinary. Because usually, as women, we flinch. It's just too hard. We bleat our vulnerability. Gabble too much about our personal lives and the toll it's taking, make excuses, give up, bow out. She doesn't play the victim, just keeps on going, audaciously blindsiding the media now and then, and for these women it's becoming an exhilarating sport to witness. 'She's such a strong role model for our daughters,' said one of them.

She's doing her job with a mental toughness reminiscent of John Howard: no matter what's thrown at them they keep on at it, with focus and tenacity and a quietly effective steeliness. She's gone through the intense media vitriol that many women in the public eye – daring to do something beyond the confines of what's expected of them – endure. The rite of passage: that predictable process of tearing down. I went through it with my novel *The Bride Stripped Bare*. It's extraordinarily lonely within the eye of the storm; you feel a loss of control over the personal narrative of your life – that no matter how many times you try explaining what you're doing, no one wants to listen. They prefer their own, sparkier, more destructive narrative. It makes a better story. Opinion's hardened into fact, gossip and downright lies become news and the overwhelming feeling is that they want to break you, make you go away, be silent, stop. You're like a fox hounded by a gaggle of fevered pack dogs who've scented blood.

A month ago the singer Lana Del Rey went through that depressingly familiar hammering; she cancelled her Oz tour following relentless criticism of her looks, talent, voice – and reinvention of her image. Yet male performers don't?

Julia Gillard doesn't crack. 'She's being held up to unrealistic standards of perfection when no one's perfect, and when many male politicians seem to have their flaws regularly on display,' said a mum. 'The tear-down Julia game is a big distraction from what she's actually doing.' Professional women don't just have to be good to get somewhere – they've got to be so damned good. There was something of the ex-lawyer in her after Kevin Rudd declared his hand; a passionate articulateness, a fire in her belly coupled with a reasoned, quietly angry determination; dare I say, something of an Atticus Finch in her demeanour. But you'd be hard-pressed to find that perception in a media who set her up as ineffectual and untrustworthy, and constantly seek tension, dissention, drama and spark in a relentless 24-hour news cycle. That disconnect between what these women are being told by headline makers and what they're perceiving is what's prompting school-gate outbursts. It's a fascinating story of one particular Australian woman and the affronted psyche of a nation, and it's still unfolding.

(Originally published in the *Weekend Australian Magazine*, 31 March 2012)

A tuning fork for the soul

What happened a decade ago? A veneration of ... what? Mystery. A veering towards it like an ocean liner subtly altering course for a new destination in the great ocean of life. Yet the destination's unknown.

Once I worked at Triple J, read *Rolling Stone*, wore black polo necks; God completely absent from that world except in the lyrics of Nick Cave. One of those pitbull atheists, a sneerer à la Dawkins. Yet occasionally I'd stumble across a church service and just ... sit; this supreme dagginess usually in some foreign place where none of the aberrant behaviour would be reported back. There was something calming about these illicit experiences. A leak through the veneer of aspirant coolness; a gentle drip, drip, through the restless, anxious, often bleakly alone 20s. I felt 'righted' by these assignations, balmed.

London. Aged 30. Life greedy, busy, grasping. The chap and I in a bedsit on Fleet Street. Gruelling night shifts. He sensed I needed something else – an anchor – for I'd always gulped the tonic of the land and we had none in our little patch of London, barely a tree. One day he walked me to St Bride's (known as 'the writers' church' because of its Fleet Street location). Soon, I found myself regularly slipping into its Sunday Evensong service; brought down into stillness by a spiritual enveloping from a service mostly sung. Those evenings were clean, the shining hours.

I don't go to church anymore. At times say no, it's ridiculous, I'm with that gentle atheist Alain de Botton on this one; tipping a hat to the graces within organised religion but not sucked in by it. I'll never be with Dawkins, thumping that believers are deluded, stupid; I've too much respect for the mysterious in life, can't turn my back on wonder. And then, sometimes, a little heart-tug. At night, standing in a room filled with the sleep of my kids, just … breathing them in. A great warmth flooding through me, an enormous, heart-swelling gratitude, and I'm closing my eyes in unstoppable thanks. And again, in the wild places, where the silence hums – Antarctica's ice desert, central Australia's sand desert, under a full butter moon – again, yes.

Sometimes I feel silted up by the great rambunctiousness of living; grubbied, depleted. Need a tuning fork back into calm. The ocean liner on its unknown path is veering towards those most shining qualities of religious practice: generosity, compassion, quiet. Perhaps that's just a process of ageing, becoming a parent, stepping into the world. I gravitate to those artists who seem spirit-filled and questing, whether they dwell within a faith or not. Marilynne Robinson, Nick Cave, Michael Ondaatje, Les Murray, Philip Larkin. Those who declare seem brazen, courageous; I admire that. Wish I had their clarity.

What I do know: that religion's a miracle of survival. That places of potent spirituality do not belong entirely to Earth and there's the wonder of that. The sites that concentrate your being in some way, if you're still and quiet within them, that soften your presence into something ceremonial and inclusive; some echo of a ritual embracing you. The tugging, the faint whisper of a tugging ...

The mystery's impenetrable. Yet still we try, nibbling away at its immensity with our religions and our science. Always attempting to harness, explain, exploit. I'm not sure I believe, but want to – need to – at times. I'm an onlooker. Not in antagonism or disdain. My spirituality is private, bound by no institution, carved from years of bitsy church-going and from the land and from giving birth, carved from the shock of kindness I see again and again in people and am deeply moved by. These attacks of Dawkins and his ilk feel like a violation in some way, but I can't explain why. Because my head's telling me they're right, it's true. Yet, yet ...

(Originally published in the *Weekend Australian Magazine*, 7 April 2012)

Just let the children grow

'Parents are much less resilient than kids now,' observed a friend recently, a respected educator, and don't we all know where she's coming from.

The hovering, indignation, anguish is all around us; some of it deeply primal, raw, unbound. I've seen examples in both UK and Australian schools as aggrieved parents go into righteous battle for their precious darlings. God help the educators; there's nothing like a modern mum on a mission. Recent tales from other schools: parents demanding a recount of a school leadership ballot – in the presence of Australian electoral officers – after their child wasn't chosen as a prefect; threats to withdraw a pupil; schools being bullied with legal action if a kid's not included in the netball/ public speaking/ soccer team.

What kind of adults are being raised here? Resilience is a necessary life skill; at its core a magnificent and moving tenacity of spirit. 'The end is nothing; the road is all,' author

Willa Cather wrote – yet some parents are trying to smooth that road to a ridiculously unnatural extent. The aim? That holy grail, the child's happiness (and perhaps their own). At all costs. Bugger the rest.

Counselling psychologist Helen McGrath says the situation's no longer balanced. 'There's been a big shift in the past decade, a real loss of parenting skills. It's child-centred parenting, which results in less resilient kids as well as parents.' In the war and postwar eras, she says, Aussie children were taught to be tough, to endure, overcome. Parents wanted their kids to be independent, good people, within a community. Over the past 10 or 15 years the message has changed. There's a lot of fear fuelled by the media, yet no evidence the world's a more frightening place. Coupled with this is peer pressure – parents criticising other parents, and moving in packs to try to remove certain teachers.

McGrath believes the 'raising self-esteem' movement is discredited because the resulting narcissism has become counterproductive – the 'I'm better than anyone else, and I will get my way' syndrome. With self-esteem hasn't come the requisite counterbalance: empathy. 'We're now teaching self-respect instead of self-esteem – i.e., what you do, how you conduct yourself, your morals. We're teaching teachers to teach students. The parents are lost.'

She thinks some of the problem lies with women having babies later. They've often had a career, know how the system works and are extremely assertive. Compare that to previous generations, when women were generally meek in the face of authority. 'Women who know how, they're the ones usually driving this new way of operating,' McGrath says, 'but they've lost logical perspective.' Blinded by their ruthless path to have their child succeed at all costs; unable to see how foolish and blinkered they appear. It strikes me how little empathy these extremely competitive women have for any other child; it's like they just don't see them – and it can result in a subtle alienating by other mothers. And am I right in thinking the extremely vocal, hovery angst can often seem most pronounced in the alpha woman who once had a professional career but is now a full-time mum? Perhaps because they've time to focus, obsessively – their active minds aren't filled up with other things. Their child's success is now theirs, too. All-consumingly.

A teacher's dream parent? 'An advocate for their child, but one who does so with courtesy,' McGrath says. 'They'll respect the teacher's right to teach. And they don't want the school to fix a friendship fallout. There are lots of normal experiences kids have to go through. Parents are feeling too much through the minds of their children; they shouldn't think they have to respond emotionally.' As Christopher Robin pointed out so wisely to Pooh, 'Promise me you'll always remember: You're braver than you believe, and stronger than you seem, and smarter than you think.' It's all part of growing up.

(Originally published in the *Weekend Australian Magazine*, 14 April 2012)

Rules of the game

'There are many ways of breaking a heart,' author Pearl S. Buck said. 'Stories were full of hearts broken by love, but what really broke a heart was taking away its dream – whatever that dream might be.' Yes, I've seen it, in men who've slipped through the cracks, and in women whose life has calcified around them to the point where they seem almost erased from their former, vivid selves. It makes me think of Elizabeth Riddell's viciously melancholic lament of late afternoon, about Australian woman of a certain age: 'This is the hour when women hear their lives go ticking by.' Imagine, the stillness in that.

Catherine Brenner is another breed of Aussie woman entirely. A former corporate lawyer with a background in finance, she's a non-executive board member of the likes of Coca-Cola Amatil, Boral and AMP, and she wants to give back by helping younger generations of Australian women get ahead. Live their dreams. Particularly within a professional environment. 'There are rules of the game that no one ever tells you. Men intuitively know them. Women have to learn them.'

Women have to support each other more. (Germaine, are you listening? It means not commenting sourly on another woman's dress sense in public. It's just ... belittling. For you.) For Brenner, it's about not undermining other women, even inadvertently. 'If a female colleague's running late, don't say, "She's stuck on the school run." You don't have to explain. Men don't want to hear it.' Her message: be professional; keep the domestic and work worlds separate.

Call bad behaviour – and good. 'If guys in the workplace are talking about a female colleague in a certain way, pull them up. It can be a light-hearted response, but let them know it's not on. Likewise, if another woman's doing well, let that be known too. Women can be incredibly reluctant to acknowledge strong performances by other women.'

Help other women, but also yourself. 'Communicate up, but not about the personal. Men are good at giving updates, letting others know what they've done and achieved. It could be just a sentence in passing, but women are often reluctant to do even this.' Yes, because we like a quieter, humbler style; we assume others will notice – when they don't, necessarily. As Eleanor Roosevelt said, 'No one can make you feel inferior without your consent.'

Be alive to opportunity. 'You have to have a go. Don't be afraid of failure. Also, toughen up in terms of moving forward. Get over it. Don't remind people of your failings and don't squander opportunities.'

Never forget the power of etiquette. 'Drop the chairman or boss a thank you note. Invest in some classy stationery, perhaps with your name on it. Don't just email a CV, print one and send a personal note. It's about distinguishing yourself.' I've seen it again and again in my writing career. Aspiring writers want advice, their work read, an in with my literary agent, a puff on their book cover – yet it's fascinating how rarely I get a thank you. I'm extremely busy; all these things take time. Gratitude is noticed, and remembered.

Brenner adds: 'Buy a fabulous suit. Not black, grey or navy. Be memorable. Pitch to your advantage.' And, 'Commit your thoughts to paper. Why you want this. It's marketing; you need to be able to explain clearly and effectively what you bring to the role.'

The message is: you shape your life. No one else. This is what it means to be a woman today. So from one inspiring Aussie chick – Ms Brenner – to another. The late, lamented Outback queen, Sara Henderson, and her philosophy of getting ahead in a man's world: 'All the strength you need to achieve anything is within you. Don't wait for a light to appear at the end of the tunnel; stride down there ... and light the bloody thing yourself.'

(Originally published in the *Weekend Australian Magazine*, 21 April 2012)

Doing it for ourselves

'More sex!' The request, courtesy of an avid 80-year-old reader who feels this column's been extremely tardy in that department of late. So babes, this one's for you.

My friend embodies the carnality of yearning, her appetites huge, life-affirming. 'If I had a man now I'd crush him!' – with her desire, her lust, her want.

In fact, why not go the whole hog and talk about the one thing we chicks are extremely reluctant to wax lyrical about – with each other, let alone the blokes. A practice that conveys spark and vividness and joy and deliciousness – but you'd never guess from the label we slap on it. Those enlightened Greeks had the right idea: *anaphlan*, they named it, which loosely translates as 'up-fire'. By the early modern age it was being sternly rebuked as 'self-pollution' and now, of course it's bleakly known as masturbation (Latin derivation: 'to defile by hand'). The female variety of said defilement is always, intriguingly, considered more of a taboo than the male. But perhaps the tide's turning. The most arresting scene in the 2011 French film, *Elles*, is a lingering close-up of Juliette Binoche's face as she pleasures herself.

But why the historical hesitation in discussing the female variety? Is there an innate delicacy at work here, a sense of protectiveness – towards men? Because, after all, it's often a safer bet, so to speak, in terms of a woman achieving orgasm. We can achieve it multiple times by doing it ourselves, be guaranteed it – not always the case with sex involving men (and they, of course, may be unaware of this absence at the heart of the female experience, because we may not be inclined to tell them). 'The majority of husbands remind me of an orang-utan trying to play the violin,' Balzac declared. And believe me, every woman who's experienced the explosive power of the clitoris dreams of finding her concert violinist – the man, or woman, who'll bring her body alive.

Sex therapists often say that the number-one complaint they hear is from women who can't orgasm during intercourse. We do not always get the man who knows what he's doing, who's assured, gentle, confident. But we can vividly imagine him. Our complaints: that our sexual partners can be too rough, impatient, off target, talkative. That they can alter the rhythm at the crucial moment – interrupting the female thought pattern, the scenario in her head which may have little to do with him, actually. Remember, gentlemen: Persistence, and Patience. It takes a woman an average 15 minutes to orgasm. Distraction will kill the moment as swiftly as a power cut in a nightclub. A woman who wants an orgasm needs to concentrate because they can be so darned elusive, so difficult to nudge out.

No one's born a lover; it has to be learnt. Women are ingenious at navigating little ways to their own, private pleasure. A century ago, Havelock Ellis reported that turn-of-the-century seamstresses were using treadle-operated sewing machines to achieve orgasms by sitting on their chair edges. A girlfriend, as a teenager, discovered the good old backyard Aussie swimming pool. 'I'd swim to the edge and find a filter hole the size of a 50c coin with water coming out at high pressure. I'd hang my feet up on the edge of the pool and the magic feeling would come within minutes.' Another mate swears by the hand-held power shower. 'The soft yet forceful jets find the right place without having to lay a finger on it. It brings a whole new meaning to going to the gym.'

Sexual pleasure is all about letting go, loosening, relaxing. 'Sex seemed to me all surrender – not the woman's to the man but the person's to the body,' Alice Munro wrote. Female masturbation doesn't strike me as bleak or sex-starved or despairingly lonely. It's just another form of surrendering; an adjunct to a healthy sex life.

(Originally published in the *Weekend Australian Magazine*, 28 April 2012)

The house that roared

The space is anointed by a golden light in this, the witching hour, but it's the curtain around it that's wondrous.

It's a curtain of sound. On this balcony with its little colt of a writing desk and its old, split-cane daybed covered by a worn Irish quilt methodically hand-stitched. Across the road is the great roar of the wind in the trees, which could be the sea pummelling nearby cliffs, you cannot tell, and later, quieter, will be the talking dark of crickets and frogs and then in the morning, obscenely early, will be the great raucous cram of birdsong, the shrills and trills and shrieks. 'Get up lazybones,' it all seems to be saying, 'there's so much life to be seizing.'

I gravitate to this space to meander with thought and work and to sleep. As do the kids. As soon as I saw it, heard it, I knew I finally had the room of my own. But like everything else in this jostling, cacophonous, brimful life, the rest of them had other ideas. The tin lids gravitate to my little sliver of a sanctuary; take turns to sleep on the old daybed every night, I think for its canopy of stars and its curtain of lovely sound.

Geophony, it's called. The great spill of sound in the natural world. How dreamy to invent a word that enters the lexicon, and soundscape recordist Bernie Krause has done just that. He can hear environments in detail; his new book is *The Great Animal Orchestra* and as I lie on this balcony I think yes, it is an orchestra, and how strange and terrifying it must have been for those first British settlers, like an alien god had created this world to astound, to terrify; it sounds like it hurts to be in this place. They came from a place of soft days, soft rain, soft light, where the morning quietly clears its throat.

Australia's not like that – it's a full roar into the day, at least where I live. I dreamt of that roar all my years in England; sounds imprinted like acid on the childhood psyche. The insistent shrill of cicadas in a wall of summer heat, the whipbirds' duet, kookaburra's glee; currawongs and magpies and cockatoos. The wind scouring the granite boulders of the high country, rain pummelling tin roofs, bush taut with sound. And the scarier stuff. A sudden rustle in an edgy dark, a growl from a tree, a koala or something else, stumbling badly into a wombat hole with heart thudding, that primal Aussie myth always close: there's something out there. The apprehension was never felt in the benign English forests.

Yet, achingly, I needed something wilder, tougher, untamed over there – there were houses and buildings too soon all the time in the countryside – wanted again a world of grand scale and melodramatic skies and spareness. In the Northern Territory I'd seen Aboriginal people who'd felt sick when they left their land and I knew something of that, too, a corrosive yearning for my land, for the geophony in my blood. I realised it's not just the blackfella who holds a monopoly on a profound and spiritual connection to this land; the craving can addle any of us. The landscape is a vast seduction. Within it I feel more like myself, the person I once was, perhaps a freer, lighter, childhood self; I'm stilled, strengthened, recalibrated.

So to this little balcony with its wondrous curtain of sound; the calm when I'm on it like a candle lit. Observing the moving heft of the seasons I'm reminded of Philip Larkin's luminous poem 'The Trees': 'Begin afresh, afresh, afresh.' As I have. This journey is my most beautiful and strange because it's about coming home. Seeing it, listening to it, with fresh eyes and ears. It's about paying attention to detail with an outsider's eye yet a heart born in this place. I've always been a neophiliac, hungrily seeking the new, yet now, bizarrely – all change. I'm content. Finally. With this, just this.

(Originally published in the *Weekend Australian Magazine*, 5 May 2012)

Body blows of love

The request is modest: a Mother's Day sleep party. 'Can I come too?' bouncy little Ollie asks. Gently I explain that a sleep party involves me, a bed and no one else – for a very long time.

Cue anguish, tears, bewilderment. Mummy all by herself? At a party he's not invited to? And he's the one who sleeps jammed up against me whenever he can, limpet-stuck, as if this is the only way he can sleep, as if he'll never let me go.

But he must at some point, of course, and how I dread that; dread it with all of them. Yet mothers, of course, let go too, some so viciously it's like a piece of ragged tin dragging through the heart. I've seen parents and children living in horror of each other's potency, of the hurt, each side knowing the other's Achilles heel too well. Seen women who haven't spoken to mothers for years even as grandchildren have arrived; heard of mother–daughter counselling instigated in utter despair; of a mother declaring to her daughter that if she had her time over she'd never have children; seen friends who've cried all the way home in the car after visiting mothers because the verbal crushing has never ceased. 'If he had learnt anything it was that family was not so much what you were given as what you were able to maintain,' novelist Anthony Doerr wrote. Sometimes, yes, it's just too hard. Yet think of the urgency in W.H. Auden's plea, 'we must love one another or die', for with those great, felling familial silences – surely the bitterest rifts of all – can come a sapping of the spirit, a corrosive bewilderment, a heaviness that's carried through life. You can't be hurt by someone you don't care about.

What I've learnt: the greatest chasm between two people is love withheld by a parent. If you want to do the most damage, try messing with that most primal of human bonds. If you want a miraculous healing, try the opposite. Love withheld, as a weapon, can lock up a life; leach confidence, esteem, strength. And wounds can freshen in middle age. A few years ago I was swamped by a great welling of grief from pre-teen years when my parents split and my father remarried soon after. I thought at the time I'd coped fine, but the fault lines ran deep. In middle age I felt suddenly, inexplicably, raw, deeply vulnerable, grieving. What was this unbearable freshness within me? It was finally cauterized by facing it square on. Asking questions. Needing responses. Accepting that no one is perfect, least of all myself. With that came release into a joy that was like sparks flying off an anvil.

As a mother myself I now know what an extraordinarily difficult task it is to be a parent or step-parent. No mother is perfect, no child. As parents we must use our power wisely, generously, with restraint and empathy and compassion. Sometimes it's bloody hard. Sometimes I feel more childish, less restrained than my kids; that they're better people than me. Motherhood is all-consuming; a condition of giving, continually. The love is voluminous, extravagant, greedy; it varnishes with light, it dulls; has me dancing around the room with exhilaration then curled exhausted on the ground, fists pressed at thudding temples, lost. No matter how much love mothers have to give we're sometimes screaming inside for solitude, peace, space. To unfurl, to replenish.

That's why, before I take my own beloved mum to lunch this weekend, I'm hoping for a sleep party. It won't last for long, the tribe will all come gleefully tumbling in (hopefully not before 10am), then I'll gather the small, bright wonder of them close and breathe them in deep. And when they leave in adulthood this giggle palace of a house will wait for them, its breath held, as I, too, will wait. For the gift of their attention. For their understanding love. Despite all the faults.

(Originally published in the *Weekend Australian Magazine*, 12 May 2012)

Tips for the time-poor

The women in the chap's office are extremely concerned. They've read about his wife's general hopelessness in the domestic department, and are rallying – offering to cook meals for the family, no less. The chap's mortified.

'Take them,' I'm begging.

'Have you no shame?'

'Nope.'

Because they're my saviour. As are the many people who responded to a recent column on domestic failings with their own tales of woe yet warmth, making me feel a lot less isolated in the imperfect-parenting stakes.

Favourite birthday idea? 'The Working Mum's Cake. A tub of ice cream tipped upside down on a plate and decorated with as much confectionery as you can. Bung on a few candles. By the time it starts to melt it'll look more home-made than ever.' Brilliant, and exactly the effect I'm after. Other tips for the time- and oven-challenged: 'Grated cheese on fish fingers.' 'Porridge with banana for dinner.' 'Apple and cheese quesadillas: Two tortillas, sliced apple, grated cheese. Whack it all in sandwich press and Sunday night's sorted.' 'The slow cooker – throw anything in and something edible will emerge.' 'Scrambled eggs, although I've been known to do boiled eggs so I don't have to wash a pan.' 'An old standby: two-minute noodles and cut-up apple.' 'Frozen spinach cooked with cottage cheese, yoghurt and nutmeg.' As one mum said, 'I have to remind myself that every meal doesn't need to be a gourmet event.' And another, 'I rarely go to great effort now because cooking better-than-average meals takes too long, requires too much washing-up and the fussy ones complain.'

Then there's the poor bloke who was a victim every school lunchtime of his mother's labour-saving innovation. 'Instead of making sandwiches on a breadboard with the inevitable spill-over of crumbs, she decided to spread out the day's newspaper. Then, directly on the newsprint, she'd make lunch. That way, afterwards, she could just wrap up the bits and throw the lot in the bin. All very ingenious. Except the bread was marked by newsprint ink and I was literally eating that day's news.' Another wrote of a lifelong aversion to choko after growing up in Newcastle (I can relate: my Newy nan had a vine and contrived to put that vile, watery vegetable into seemingly everything). 'Mum, exercising all her "meat and three veg" cooking skills, boiled the green choko pieces – think boiled zucchini, only more anaemic-tasting to the power of 10. The name says it all: choko. As a result of this childhood trauma whenever I stumble over them now I feel seasick.'

The time-saving ingenuity of Australia's mothers extends far beyond the kitchen. Nit-prevention tips: 'Store brushes in the freezer' and 'the little buggers hate dirty hair and gel'. This one sounds more promising: 'From my mum – "put on your tomorrow clothes"; i.e. dress kids at night in clothes for the next day. They're only going to sleep and all my boys look like they slept in their clothes anyway. So who's to know that this time it's true? School polo shirts are perfectly resilient. Saves time in the a.m., and saves on washing.'

New discoveries: baby in high chair in front of the telly, watching *The Voice*, rapt, with the other kids, while mum's tidying up after dinner. When writing: baby in net-enclosed trampoline with kitchen utensils. Perfect playpen, and it might just instil an interest in cooking because, after all, the troupe needs training up. ('No, not by you, please,' the chap's pleading.)

A reader suggests that a compendium of embarrassing parent stories should be mandatory in all hospital bounty bags given to new parents. 'It'd prevent much early parenting angst and give people a reason to laugh, which is so often needed among the domestic disaster.' Oh yes. And this was a common theme among the responses: families that are time-poor but giggle-rich. 'We do laugh, sing and dance a lot – that's gotta count for something, right?' Absolutely my friend, absolutely.

(Originally published in the *Weekend Australian Magazine*, 19 May 2012)

Advance, Australians

The dream of glorious otherness.

It's what inspires so many Aussie expats to stride hungrily into the world. They yearn for something else; a release, a remaking, an escape; there's a great dynamism to that yearning that propels them forward voraciously – and extremely successfully. They're not going to atrophy with that visceral, urgent potency within them. And coupled with the Aussie's can-do mentality, well, what a potency it can be in foreign markets.

I saw it all around me in the exile years: Aussies in love with the great zoom of life, elsewhere, and wanting to seize it while they can. It was often, intriguingly, born of small places – outback towns, suburbia's quietness – as if the very narrowness of those judgmental little worlds was the flint to fly.

Never underestimate the kick in the youthful compulsion to create a different self beyond what family/ locality/ life has moulded for you. Couple it with that bolshy Aussie attitude of 'why shouldn't I do this, no one says I can't' and the results can be spectacular.

'What is that feeling when you're driving away from people and they recede on the plain till you see their specks dispersing? It's the too-huge world vaulting us, and it's good-bye. But we lean forward to the next crazy venture beneath the skies,' Jack Kerouac wrote in *On the Road*.

They were of a type, those kids leaning forward all around me in exile. Once I gave a speech as a novelist to young Aussies at Cambridge; some of us went for a drink afterwards and I marvelled at these bright young things, many not from flash schools in the Big Smoke but places like Broken Hill or a Tassie hamlet. It made me so proud of Australia; they got to this hallowed institution through sheer grit and brilliance, seemed so shiny and questing, so poised for the future.

And I could discern the ingrained bluntness and practicality of the Antipodean childhood; the mums all those years ago telling them to just pick themselves up and get on with it, don't muck about, just do it; the dads telling them to get out there and make something of themselves with hard yakka and a smile on their faces – and always look out for your mates.

They're valued, highly, these Aussies overseas. It's our greatest natural resource, our shiniest export to the world. That smile, that enthusiasm, that breezy, can-do grit; that ease in stepping into something beyond the comfort zone. They do vaultingly ambitious things because no one's told them they can't; they've not been clamped down by a suffocating sense of class, of hierarchical place determined by birth. It's a refreshing fearlessness. Who says we can't do it? If it doesn't work out we can always go home, or try something else. But it just might …

Take my mate Kylie Morris, the Maitland chick who told her BBC bosses they needed a bureau in Gaza and set one up – they then sent her on to Iraq and Afghanistan. Overseas we all felt bolder and braver than we'd ever been back home; all the Aussies around us were do-ers and it was infectious. We brought to our new lands a restless, cheeky, larrikin energy, a feeling we could be anything here.

Serafina Maiorano is the CEO of Advance, an international networking organisation for Aussie expats. Our nation's USP in the global expat market? 'We're known as go-getters,' she says, 'adaptable, energetic, positive, innovative, hard-working yet easy-going, highly educated.'

I'm excited to be raising my kids as Aussies because of where it may lead them as adults.

And I'll never stifle the sense of yearning that may bloom in them – to be someone else, somewhere else – agonising as that is for a mum to acknowledge. But necessary. As Ben Okri wrote in 'To an English Friend in Africa': 'Learn to free yourself from all things/ That have moulded you/ And which limit your secret and undiscovered road.'

(Originally published in the *Weekend Australian Magazine*, 26 May 2012)

First among equals

Were you your parents' favoured child? The least? Is there a rueful melancholy even thinking about that?

The damage can work both ways – if there was a golden sibling beside you, or if you basked in the glow. The perception, rightly or wrongly, can stain a life; we can spend our whole existence trying to counter our parents' biases, developing ingenious ways to be noticed – or just giving up.

My father, canny old thing he is, is always teasing his seven kids that one of us is the chosen one, but he's never saying which. It keeps us all on our toes. He says only one has ever asked, 'Is it me, Dad?' Is it a surprise it was the eldest, the firstborn son? I have a giggle about that. Floating somewhere around the middle of the brood, I just wouldn't presume. Studies show it's most likely the firstborn or the last; a mother's more inclined to favour a son, a father a daughter. God knows with Bob Gemmell. I strongly suspect he doesn't actually have a chosen one although studies say that's usually not the case.

One from the University of California Davis concluded that 65 per cent of mums and 70 per cent of dads had a preference for one child and in most cases it was the eldest.

My alliance with Dad, jostling with so many other disparate personalities, is now founded on what I think is the secret of any good relationship (not least a marriage): laughter. Combating with a light heart. It's my survival tactic and whether it works or not I don't know, he's not saying. We all define ourselves through sibling difference and Dad said to me once that the squeaky wheel on the bike always gets the attention ... perhaps trying to explain why he's never paid me much notice, comparatively, in the great rush of life. To him, I just didn't need it. It used to hurt, violently, as I mistook love for attention, but now as a parent I understand – we can only fight so many spot-fires at once and the love can still be there. Unspoken.

Anna Campion, filmmaker sister of Jane, said once, 'Our parents believed that if you wanted a child to do well, you'd just ignore them.' I recognise that. All my attempts at achieving when young were perhaps a tenacious ploy to be noticed, fuelled by a subliminal anger at being ignored.

Apparently favouritism is a biological instinct. Parents tend to lean towards the strongest, healthiest child because nature dictates that it's the one who'll be the most successful, reproductively, at widening the gene pool.

I don't have a favourite. They've all clung to me like wet plastic bags slicked around a tree and I've held each one in return fiercely, voraciously – equally. Yes, there's the absolute wonder of the firstborn as he blazes the path for the rest of them, let alone his parents, in terms of how we navigate the whole child-rearing thing. ('He's the one we're experimenting on,' the chap and I often say – poor thing.) I craved the daughter next, succumbing to an obscene, ugly bout of narcissism. There was a flash of disappointment when the midwife declared 'It's a boy!' – but then I saw this most scrumptious of babies and have been passionately in love ever since. It's like nature made Son Number Two so vividly adorable to guarantee the intensity of the wonder all over again (or maybe our son's just very canny).

Narcissistic craving still raging, I googled 'gender selection/ female/ diet' . Ate yoghurt until I could no longer bear it. Got the girl. Wonder, delight, chuff. And finally the wee interloper, crashing most impertinently into his parents' middle ages just as we were lightening, loosening, climbing back into the world – and sleeping the bliss of uninterrupted nights. He should be resented but he's become like a medieval kissing post; cuddled, kissed, by all of us, endlessly. Yet I cannot say he's loved anymore than the rest … honestly.

(Originally published in the *Weekend Australian Magazine*, 9 June 2012)

The solace of solitude

Novelist Will Self declares dinner parties should last only 90 minutes. 'Because I don't drink I get bored at dinner parties. I don't mind people drinking, as long as they aren't falling over, but in the past 10 years or so, if you don't drink, you really want a dinner party to last about an hour and a half.' US *Vogue* editor Anna Wintour rarely stays at a party longer than 20 minutes. Both these stances I admire, envy, perhaps because the wolfish hunger for solitude is lean and mean in me – as it is in many writers, despite that modern-day circus tent of literary festival and author lunch.

'I feel a real horror of people closing over me,' Katherine Mansfield wrote in her journal in 1914. It's a horror that damn well yowls inside me whenever too many demands nibble into my serenity. And the ability to cleave precious moments of solitude from within the great whoosh of family and professional life is becoming increasingly difficult. The ultimate social nightmare? A party a long way away, in a place devoid of taxis, fully reliant on someone else for a lift home. Someone who lingers, agonisingly, over one more drink, one more anecdote, the bloated evening yawning on … and on.

For grizzly old curmudgeons like myself solitude is never overcomplicated, stressful, loud – and most certainly never lonely. You can be much lonelier at Christmas within the midst of a family you don't quite belong to or within a marriage that's atrophied into indifference. Aloneness can have a vast restorative power; there's something spiritual and consoling to it. It's space for your mind to uncurl. Those poor, restless souls who draw no comfort from solitude; I wish them the gift of solace from it. I'm all at sea, lost, if time by myself can't be carved from the great cram of everything else. And then, in the lovely, glittery alone, a door opens to possibility and it's when novel ideas sneak in, titles roar with their rightness, surprising character arcs veer me back into excitement over a project that hasn't been singing. It's my brewing house for creativity, my Laboratorium of Wonder. Oh, the grace of those shining hours!

Plotinus called it 'the flight of the alone to the alone', yet as a mother it carries an enormous burden of guilt. You can't do it all, be it all, within the rush of modern motherhood; something has to give within that great, exhausting triumvirate of family/ work/ social life – and it's the latter I've sacrificed for now. Yet the clincher, as precious little jewels of alone are gleaned, is the knowing that the more solitude I filch, the less I shout. At everyone else. Within the thick of motherhood the restorative power of aloneness feels like a private miracle, every time. It doesn't happen much – but it's when things are done.

Novelist Marilynne Robinson describes herself as 'a solitary', but tempers it. 'My solitary life is not exclusively a solitary life. I like to come out and look at the world and talk with people and all that sort of thing … It's just a matter of trying to find a liveable balance.'

I, too, scuttle out into the world for the odd party or dinner where my car's close, for escape, but I've become more courageous with age at slipping off, unobtrusively, when ready. And is it just me or does the social world now feel a little more shouty, in your face, raucous? Everyone's so eager to talk at you, over the top of you, cram in their two bob's worth, compete with their hilarious anecdotes – but to actually, quietly, enquire? To deeply listen? Is the art of conversation morphing?

I leave you with a recent observation from director Mike Nichols, broadcaster Diane Sawyer's husband. 'One of the things that fascinates me about Diane, who goes all over the world all the time – she's in Afghanistan, she's in Iraq, she's everywhere and then back in a day and a half – is that no one ever asks her about what she saw … people, by and large, would rather be talking than listening.'

(Originally published in the *Weekend Australian Magazine*, 16 June 2012)

Back in the balance

Are you spending less? I am, and it feels like a lot of people around me are, too.

It's OK now to declare 'I'm just not going into shops like I used to', or 'I don't buy things anymore'. Note, also, that word 'things'. Because looking back, what on earth did we spend all that money on? During those gluttonous, glary years of the early 21st century, when it felt like the bubble would never burst? And now, some kind of seismic shift is under way. Can you feel it?

A correcting, perhaps, in our spending habits, the way we live. A quietness is taking over.

It feels like we're all contracting, becoming more cautious, that we're all squirrels storing nuts for a coming winter we suspect will be long and hard. Like Antarctica crisp in the air of Tassie, this chill wind from other worlds is steely. What's next for crippled Europe? Will we be dragged into it?

Coupled with that, I suspect, is a growing revulsion over the monstrous excesses of several short years ago. I succumbed. My world was stained by it. We lived in a London pocket hosting two extremes of living – bankers in their rarefied, six-storey villas, and the people rubbing up hard alongside them, in council estates erected on the bomb sites of villas flattened in the war (let's just say we were the squeezed middle). We were surrounded by families with four cars, 'one just for the motorway'; weekday nannies for each child as well as a weekend nanny; and burning Guy Fawkes effigies that wore Burberry coats. I've never felt more trapped, anxious, sour, than when living among this. It all felt so removed from the real world. These people made their money by exploiting other people's money – and expected to be rewarded with sickening sums of moolah for doing so. It wasn't creative, ennobling, inspiring in any way – and certainly wasn't cool. Who aspires to be a banker now?

In attempting to keep up with the Joneses the chap and I lived a precarious existence. Then something extraordinary happened.

We split open our lives to fate by mutually agreeing to quit our London lives and up sticks for a return to Australia. Almost instantaneously we felt a great weight lifting. An incredible lightness of being; an exhilaration. That the years of living on the edge and foolish competitiveness would all, suddenly, evaporate. And ahead, the gift of a simpler, sparer life. One that might still be beholden to monthly mortgage payments but would feel far less fretful, anxious, clenched. Suddenly

I felt stronger than I had for years. Free. I'd forgotten that rupture can be good, cleansing, correcting. It was a hugely constructive time and we've lived with that sense of frugality ever since. Three kids now share a bedroom, the watch is a Swatch and the car's a Kia. We've never been happier.

Who at the moment is living gracefully with excessive wealth? My favourite: J.K. Rowling. She made her money by exploiting neither people nor land, and her large charitable donations have helped to boot her out of the ranks of the world's dollar billionaires this year, according to *Forbes* magazine. Then there's our own mining billionaires. Plundering our common wealth yet bleating over having to pay the mining tax on the back of eye-watering profits. To me it feels petulant, juvenile, a massively greedy and ugly dummy-spit; and out of step with sentiment brewing in the rest of the world. Warren Buffett calling for higher taxes for America's super rich; a French group, including L'Oreal heiress Liliane Bettencourt and Total's Christophe de Margerie, doing the same. Our Aussie lot feel glaringly at odds with a collective global consciousness gathering force, a sense of responsibility that's being voiced, astonishingly, from the rarefied top. Congratulations, Gina, you're now the wealthiest woman in the world. My question for you is, what on Earth are you going to do with it?

(Originally published in the *Weekend Australian Magazine*, 23 June 2012)

A bush picnic

'The fields are like sand, Mummy.' A poet! And this from the girl who was named after that triumvirate of creative Aussie chicks – the Theas Astley, Proctor and Mackellar.

My wee Londoner, used to a Cotswold countryside of benign green, is seeing the Aussie bush for the first time. Saucer eyes. At grass the colour of the sheep that are on it. Fallen dead trees like sunbathers. Skippy headless by the road. 'What are those black things?' That would be cows. 'Look at the cows with blankets on!' Er no, those would be horses.

'Where are all the sheep going in that truck?' Silence. Have to think about that one. 'On an adventure, just like us,' the chap jumps in, and Thea claps her hands – we're off on a most exciting one, 'inside Australia'! To a property stretching back 150 years, all high on glee – it's been a while since we've had a break, held hostage as we are by the kids' relentless routine of weekend sport.

At the property, so much for our little Londoners to absorb. Cattle grids. Tin windmills. Tourniquet kits in the jeep. Baths the colour of tea, dam water as soft as silk. A tumble of sheep dogs. An airstrip and petrol bowser, a rest stop for the bush fire brigade, and a creek still bearing the scars of flooding: the contradictions of bush life. An 11-year-old station daughter who plays Bach on the piano – and drives the jeep. A disused pub that carries memories of bullockies and drays and ingeniously, as modern as tomorrow, has a fenced-off bit of veranda for the pioneering kids and their peace-scrabbling parents (Thea instinctively heads into it). A bush picnic in a neighbour's paddock 'just up the road' – an hour's drive away. Snags in bread and lamb chops in fingers; galumphing appetites. Silence that's a presence. Light that assaults you and how I dreamt of it during exile – wanting to wear sunshine, achingly, under all those English clouds grazing the rooftops like the bellies of cows. On a hill crest the chap and I lie flat on our backs under the tall, hurting blue and breathe it in deep – air that is home.

Yet there's a melancholy to this world now – that Australia no longer rides on the back of it. It's increasingly hard to get the sons and daughters of the land to take over these places. They know better. Opportunity's elsewhere and the work's daunting; seven days a week, dawn to dusk and beyond. The owners can't afford to sit back anymore; they need to toil as hard as the people they're hiring – and there aren't as many of those, with labour costs high and returns not as great. Our dear friends are selling up; the landowner's ageing and his daughter's got an overseas boarding school to get to. She wants to be a lawyer. Increasingly, foreign investors are buying into properties like this, or city slickers wanting a weekender. Mainly older people attended the paddock picnic: women in jeans and pearls, men in moleskins and RMs, venerable families from the land. But it feels, sadly, like a kind of generational majesty is fading here, waning.

Meanwhile, we revelled in it all. This despite the chap's first-night declaration that my new stripy pyjamas made me look like a huge tube of toothpaste, and he wasn't going near me. But the next day, under that glorious sky, he nudged close as we lay in the sun and remembered the people we once were. Refound a tenderness. What a circuit-breaker a holiday can be! We'd forgotten how replenishing a release from the daily grind is.

As for Thea? Not so keen on her name anymore. After an exhilarating holiday of abandoned pubs and bush-bashing and dogs and dirt she's declared she's a tomgirl. New name, Harry (don't ask; we can't explain it either). Forthcoming fifth birthday: a mud party. Ah, the Aussie bush. It gets to all of us, eventually.

(Originally published in the *Weekend Australian Magazine*, 30 June 2012)

Shelf life

'Excuse me, I'm researching a new novel and am wondering if the library has any books on …' (a spreading blush) '… sex.'

'Oh yes, you'll find them in two sections. Under P for Pleasure, and F for Flagellation.'

(A pause.) 'I'll take Pleasure.'

This conversation really happened. About a decade ago, in my beloved London Library that most wilfully does not subscribe to the standard Dewey decimal system – and is wonderfully distracting because of it. The labyrinthine building in St James's Square arrests time, dragging you into its rich, dark depths and holding you captive. There are always diversions stretching into chapters and sometimes entire books in golden days of vivid, reviving lost-ness. I met the chap there once, waited at the entrance for half an hour before he appeared. 'Sorry, got lost in philology,' he explained in the tone of someone held up by a kindly, elderly woman who just wouldn't let him go. He'd accumulated a coating of dust from shelves he'd been trying to extricate himself from. 'Getting lost in philology' is now a catchphrase between us, meaning 'to lose one's way, for some time, in an unfamiliar but deeply endearing place'.

The library was founded in 1841 and quickly became a toolhouse for writers. Dickens had two cartloads of books sent to him for *A Tale of Two Cities*. E.M. Forster took out two life subscriptions. Virginia Woolf wrote in her diary, 'L[eonard] found D[esmond MacCarthy] at the London Library; together they looked up the word f--- in the slang dictionary, and were saddened and surprised to see how the thumbmarks of its members were thick on the page.'

The design is wondrous, the stacks held aloft by five storeys of iron grilles (women should avoid skirts). It's like acquainting yourself with the bold skeleton of a beautiful building. If you're soft-shod, the gratings thrum. Strips of fluorescent tubing cast baubles of light here and there, and above and below you readers sit or squat, engrossed, each isolated in their little circle of light. When I left London for good I relinquished my membership. It broke my heart.

I dreaded returning to the imagined beigeness of the Australian library; the panic heightened soon after arrival when Mum delivered several milk-crates of items she'd been minding for, er, decades. In one: a library book on Sylvia Plath, borrowed when I was 17 (too terrified to return it, 17 was a long time ago). But actually, something quite magical is happening to Australia's libraries. A recognition that these temples of the written word should be cherished, modernised, protected; that they fulfil a necessary function in this increasingly rushing world. They promote stillness. Quiet. Reflection. Thank goodness for enlightened councils that keep these institutions vibrant. Our local library has glass doors flung wide to the water, cool couches and glamorous light fittings. It's a heart-lifter of a space. Its toddler singalongs are regularly booked out, instilling in future readers a cherishing they'll hopefully carry through life.

So, libraries are being enchantingly revived, sales of fountain pens are reportedly rising worldwide and the drug du jour in London is, apparently, snuff. Something's going on – an experimentation with the past, a craving to claim it before it's gone. There's a proposal to turn Sydney's Customs House into Australia's first 24-hour library. I love this idea. Libraries are embracing the cool factor; they're becoming sexy sanctuaries of thought that force you to pause in the mad rush of life. A deep, deep peace plumed through me in the London Library and I feared I'd never be able to replicate that feeling in Australia but I do, oh I do, in my little local library.

It's a cherished hub – just like that deeply eccentric institution in St James's Square.

(Originally published in the *Weekend Australian Magazine*, 7 July 2012)

Never too late

The intelligence is alarming: reports of sequinned shorts on mums over summer at the kindy end of school, bare shoulders, cleavage.

That instead of meeting for coffee they meet for ... walks. Brisk ones. In gym gear. And in five short years, among all this effulgent youthfulness will be ol' grandma here, dropping off wee Jago on his first day. Yep, the one who began her career with typewriters and cassettes. So old she no longer recognises the starlets on the cover of *Vanity Fair* – such a painful barometer of middle age – and not only doesn't recognise them, but buys the magazine not for the cover story but the boring articles around it. The joys of ageing.

A year ago, I wrote about having a baby at an obscene age. The affronted rallied. A Perth obstetrician, Dr Barry Walters, wrote most sternly that planning a pregnancy beyond the age of 39 was 'entirely self-centred'. Why is it so often men who are enraged by the very thought of older mothers; women who dare, perhaps, to desire careers and autonomy before settling into parenthood? Surrounding all the late mothers I know is nothing but gobsmacked, soaring shock – of the joyous kind. For these are often mums who've been hampered by years just slipping away, or a Mr Right never quite materialising, or an unimaginable grief involving futile attempts to conceive, or repeated miscarriages. Oh, it hurts. I've lost two babies. The pain was enormous, ragged, yowling. 'Cry and cry again,' said a sensitive radiographer, 'it's a bereavement.' Yes.

So, a year in, a report from the coalface of late motherhood. We're not advocating leaving it so late but for a lot of us, it felt like our body's last hurrah before the wintriness of menopause sets in, like an Indian summer bursting into miraculous, shocking, gleeful warmth.

Was it the Pill's introduction that caused this modern unease over older mothers, combined with a reproving, mostly male medical fraternity? Before this, women had babies right through the years of fertility because that's what they did. Charles Darwin's wife had her last at 48.

Of course I'm tired, but I was tired with the firstborn 12 years ago. And then it was all compounded by the shock of the new. I was less in control; horrified at this other, exhausted woman who occasionally slipped out; despairing at the vast shunting-aside from a former self that felt almost rude, shocking. Now I'm no longer trying to fit it all in and getting frustrated when I can't. With us older mums the relationship's often settled, as are finances and, crucially, career. We're more empowered. In the words of a fellow oldie-mum, 'We've got balls now.' We're calmer. More confident. More resilient emotionally and more relaxed. It only helps the child. My parenting attitude now is: whatever feels right. Increasingly, that's what chimes with nature.

At Jago's birth I was classified as hugely at risk because of age. Would be induced on the due date for the child's safety. Was reluctant to start that day on a drip being pumped with hormones. Tried a cervical sweep, which made me think of nothing so much as being in the back of a Cronulla panel van – painful, intrusive, awkward. It didn't work. What was my body telling me? To walk. I did, on the beach. And Victorian women used to clean floors to bring on labour – I ended up on all fours, miming scrubbing. Reader, I scrubbed that baby out of me. The contractions started soon after. Jago was born in less than an hour, half an hour before his due date. I was 44.

The affronted say it's too risky, selfish, stupid, that we're no role model. But don't be talked out of it if you're trying. I'm giddied by the thought of Jago, eating him with kisses just to hear that giggle, so life-affirming, wondrous, miraculous. He's keeping me young. Dr Walters, take note.

(Originally published in the *Weekend Australian Magazine*, 21 July 2012)

Writing's on the wall

When was the last time you wrote something by hand? Something meaty, weighty, enduring.

Can you remember? Don't be alarmed if you can't; a new study says the typical adult hasn't scribbled anything down for almost six weeks. We're increasingly using keypads and touch phones to convey messages; address books are disappearing; birthday greetings are emailed. Is handwriting going the way of tying shoelaces? A study by online stationer Docmail found the average adult last wrote something by hand 41 days ago, and one in three hadn't had a reason to write anything 'properly' for more than six months.

Coupled with this is a dramatic decline in quality. My own writing's now somewhat tramp-like – scruffy, bitsy, blowsy and understood by no one, including yours truly. Ideas are jotted in a notebook but the hand's barely legible. I'm ashamed, especially when thinking back to the rigorous cursive script of my convent school days – a hand as beautifully starched and neat as a wimple.

My sons learnt a lovely cursive script in their London school, yet that discipline doesn't seem to be enforced here. They're back to printing. Does it really matter if that's what works for them? Will future generations barely use a pen and paper at all (let alone shoelaces)? Will they forget how to write?

But there's an opportunity here. If you want to give pause, be noticed – write by hand. And this is where another recent phenomenon comes in: sales of fountain pens are soaring. Parker, proud manufacturer since 1888, says there's been a worldwide resurgence over the past five years; rival Lamy says turnover increased by more than five per cent in 2011. Yet figures for ballpoints are stable. Why? Possibly because they drive us bananas. In supermarkets the stationery section's always perused – favourite bit by far – the pens scoured, searching for that elusive keeper. Oh, the frustration. They're either too light, too spidery, hideously scratchy or run out too fast. So many just feel cheap, ephemeral, like they're not trying hard enough.

Then there's the fountain pen. I've had my old Waterman for years. Bought from the most sublime of department stores, Bon Marché in Paris, which feels fitting in that nation of readers who haven't yet embraced the e-book with the vigour of other countries. Béatrice de Plinval, from jeweller Chaumet, writes entirely in sepia ink. Fabulously glamorous – but where does one find said ink in Oz?

There's something deeply pleasurable about my black-lacquered Waterman. I love the solid click of its lid, as satisfying as the crisp snap of a 1950s handbag. Love its weightiness – it purrs reassurance, respectability. The pen slips across the page in a velvety glide, giggles away from me – and makes me want to write more, more. It doesn't snag or catch or scratch at the paper, its design is ingeniously enduring, it's cheap to run. Then there's the tobacco tin it lives in, a history of a writing life in that battered box. Bought while fleeing a traumatic jilting several months before I was due to walk down the aisle, my heart a howl of grief. I'd jumped into my old Holden ute and headed back to the place I loved most fiercely – Alice Springs. Stopped at a junk shop in Broken Hill and picked up this tin, the beautifully exact length of the pen. It's lived snug in it ever since, along with the writer's tools of red pen, pencil and rubber. Just the act of opening the box is pleasurable; there's a little stirring of aaaah, now I'm doing what I really want to do.

It feels like handwriting's becoming more exclusive, personal, treasured in this fast, throwaway screen-world. The cherishing of fountain pens is a lovely adjunct to that. As we left London for good, my eldest son was given a smart silver pen by a mate. Both their names are engraved on it. It's a keeper, that one.

(Originally published in the *Weekend Australian Magazine*, 28 July 2012)

Spare the blushes

Would you ever read Pauline Reage's visceral little tome, *Story of O*, openly, on a train?

A generation ago, a decade, even last summer, the answer for most of us would have been a resounding, 'God no.' And now, all change. For over this winter we've witnessed an astonishing loosening of the corsetry of decorum, a rectitude that's bound many of us all of our lives. Honesty is spilling out; women's intensely vivid, secret inner lives are being openly discussed – and those inner lives feel surprisingly universal. It's all down to one book, of course – *Fifty Shades of Grey* – and it's shifting something, profoundly, in the reading habits of women.

Edith Wharton's mother forbade her from reading any novels until after she married; Virginia Woolf had a home education which involved wading through her father's library. Neither went to school or university. Their fine minds were shaped by what their parents ordered them to read.

A history of women's reading is often a history of the suppressed, controlled reader; from time immemorial there's been a strand of thinking, across cultures, that allowing women to read whatever they want leads to independence, dangerous thoughts, illicit actions, depravity. Juvenal, in the 1st century, wrote of ridiculous and repulsive female scholars; an 18th-century French pamphlet thundered that women suffered convulsions and vapours if they read; and recently British journalist Christina Lamb wrote of Afghan women discussing books covertly, avidly, within the homely disguise of the sewing circle.

Now we have women across the western world openly discussing E.L. James's *Fifty Shades* trilogy, which read like female porn mags. I realised something extraordinary was afoot when a buttoned-up school mum declared, 'It's doable. The sex in them. I kept on thinking, "Yeah, I could go there."' It felt astonishing that she of all people would be saying this. Something's happened in our reading psyche, fast. There's talk of a baby boom next year brought on by the books; of Saturday afternoons at Bunnings suddenly becoming a lot more giggly, spicy.

It's been said *Fifty Shades* has the e-book revolution to thank for its success: women can download it knowing that no one will have any idea what they're reading. But the phenomenon is bigger than that: it's about the fact that we openly devour and discuss this type of book now without any trace of embarrassment. I've even slipped my *Story of O* from its bookshelf purgatory in a darkened corner – it doesn't need to be so coy. It's such an explosive piece of writing, yet tender too. I still remember the tug in the belly, the heated flush upon first reading it. As French author Catherine Millet wrote, 'For me, a pornographic book is functional, written to help you get excited.' Thanks to *Fifty Shades* Western women of all persuasions can now be declaratory, shameless, about these things.

A mere 10 years ago, when I wrote *The Bride Stripped Bare*, it felt like a different world. My follow-up to it, *With My Body*, came out last year and even then the landscape felt different – 'It's not the sort of book I'd read on a train,' said a mate who'd swiped it from his wife. But now, astonishingly quickly, all change.

The universality of the female response to a tale of submission, both in *Story of O* and *Fifty Shades*, is intriguing. What does it tell us about the raw underbelly of the female psyche – what do a lot of women really want? It may be something never articulated.

Yet E.L. James seems to have, for many women. 'The whole business of eroticism is to destroy the self-contained character of the participators as they are in their normal lives,' Georges Bataille wrote. It feels like a lot of readers have had a door opened to them – and wondrously, boldly, they're walking through it. Or at least considering it …

(Originally published in the *Weekend Australian Magazine*, 4 August 2012)

Dust yourself down

Ah, the F-word. That fractious, tetchy, emotional little word that pops up again and again in school-gate conversations.

It feels like fear of it is increasing not only among young people but even more so, perhaps, among their anxious, hovering parents. We're talking Failure. Not my precious little darling! Imagine the long-term psychological damage! Certificates for all, please! But should we be encouraging this cushioning from one of the most fundamental fuels of a successful life? Brisbane Girls Grammar doesn't think so. It's introduced a course for first-year high school students that teaches them the importance of risk-taking, how to build resilience and, crucially, not seeing failure as a setback but as a way to grow.

Educators are waking up to the fact that a terror of failing is becoming a constraining problem, particularly among girls. In February England's Wimbledon High School held a 'Failure Week' for its female students. The emphasis was on the value of having a go as opposed to playing it safe and possibly achieving less. Headmistress Heather Hanbury wanted to show 'it is completely acceptable and normal not to succeed at times in life … The girls need to learn how to fail well – and how to get over it … Fear of failing can be really crippling and stop the girls doing things they really want to do.'

Girls can be so easily crushed; stymied by those particularly female traits of perfectionism, lack of self-esteem, hatred of criticism, fear of speaking out, fear of making a fool of oneself. But failure can set anyone back. I've become inured to it as I've aged simply because I've become so used to it. From cupcakes never turning out right to abandoned novels that never took off, phones not ringing after interviews and most recently, flinching little moments of failure in parenting. ('Can you go away again, Mummy?' declared one of the little darlings after I'd returned recently from a business trip.) But what I've learnt – slowly, painfully, angrily, beautifully – is that failure's a gift. In some way. Always. Because it's never the end of the world; you're always learning something in the process and it's often veering you onto a different, better, stronger path.

As Henry Ford said, 'Failure is simply the opportunity to begin again, this time more intelligently.' If we've got the courage to pick ourselves up and try and try again, well, that's where magnificence comes into play, those moving life-narratives we all respond to.

Take Winston Churchill. Ranked last in his primary school class, his headmaster wrote: 'He is a constant trouble to everybody … He cannot be trusted to behave himself anywhere.' Only on his third attempt did Churchill pass the entrance exam to Sandhurst. But crucially, he was always a risk-taker. And by nature, those are the people most comfortable with failure. 'Success is not final, failure is not fatal: it is the courage to continue that counts,' he said.

The test of a person's character is in how they react to failure. Over these past two weeks [during London's Olympic Games] we've seen tears, bewilderment and blame after losses – even after coming second. I was in England for Andy Murray's defeat in the Wimbledon final; it felt like the entire nation was watching, fervently wishing for triumph. They needed this. His shining, heartfelt speech in defeat was beautifully self-deprecating and generous to his victor. In that moment the dour Scot became endearingly human to me; he was ennobled by his grace.

I could suddenly see the arc of a splendid narrative. Remember, in the sting of defeat people are watching. It's then that we empathise – for we've all failed – and it's then that there's the potential to gauge the human spirit at its most moving and magnificent. By all means fail, just don't become a lesser person because of it. Pick yourself up. Show us your courage. Endure. We all crave that narrative, if not in ourselves then in others. It's human nature.

(Originally published in the *Weekend Australian Magazine*, 11 August 2012)

Lifting our game

'Just put on your big girl's pants!'

Thus yelled a beloved British mate to her home team during those early, despairing days of the Olympics, when Team GB was inspiring front-page splashes along the lines of WANTED: GOLD MEDAL. The mate's choice turn of phrase was pleading for all the grit and brusqueness and tenacity associated with the traditional bluestocking's eminently sensible undergarments: i.e., just get on with the job and do it.

Which they did. Magnificently. I saw the seeds of that glory four years ago. The scene: an inner London state primary, brimming with kids more interested in the Notting Hill Carnival than sport. One day an alien force visited: sporting officials. All the six-year-olds got on the floor, bent over knees, flexed toes.

My boy's mate was pulled out; the one who'd never kicked a footy, let alone held a cricket bat in his life. 'Son, we're going to make you a diver.' 'But I can't even swim!' (Not uncommon among inner-city Londoners.) 'We'll teach you.' They did. Because they'd discerned something in his strength and flexibility. The goal: the 2020 Olympics.

The little man eventually pulled out; the sheer grind and competitiveness wasn't for him or his family, but it was a lesson in far-sighted preparation from a nation not usually associated, until recently, with the glories of modern Olympic sport.

John Coates, president of our own Olympic Committee, lamented that Australia has to think harder about sport in schools. 'You've got … to look at what the rest of the world is doing. High performance in other countries has gone past us.'

I got a sinking feeling about Team Australia during the opening ceremony; there was something a little too cocky yet haphazard about the way they were all walking in their ranks (too kind a word), about the way they were 'bunched'. It all felt a tad too ragged, yet bolshy; such a fatal, hubristic combination.

There's another area that intrigues in terms of Australia and how the rest of the world is preparing for the future. One of the reasons our family left Britain was because the kids were galloping into the trauma of the 11-plus exams. All around us were children being tutored, some of them three times a week; ten- and 11-year-olds with anxiety rashes on their faces, having breakdowns, hating parents. It just didn't feel right in terms of how kids should be raised; as one Londoner remarked, 'It's child abuse.' Yet we now know that tutoring is rampant not only in London but across New York, Seoul, Shanghai – and in Australia's main cities, too.

Our eldest son's taken competitive exams this year for high-school entry, and what's intrigued us are stories of kids who've been tutored since kindergarten, who go to not one but three coaching colleges a week. How is this skewing results? What kind of adults are being raised here? An educator tells me the flipside is rarely discussed: breakdowns, suicides, tender young psyches imploding under the enormous pressure to succeed.

But how to compete? Some of the nation's top selective state schools have demographics that are 90 per cent Asian. It'll be intriguing to see how these kinds of figures – this disconnect in cultural discipline and work ethic – impacts upon Australia in generations to come. Will there be an Anglo class of achievement that sits quite differently to that ingrained, tenacious drive of the Asian student?

Will we all be pulled up by example? There's been a lot of talk recently of the world leaving us behind in sport, but we have to look at other areas, too. That lovely, laconic Aussie attitude of 'she'll be right, mate' – seen abundantly in our team's stroll during the opening ceremony – may not be enough in this increasingly competitive, internationalised world that's stepping up its game all around us. In every arena, not just the sporting.

(Originally published in the *Australian Weekend Magazine*, 18 August 2012)

Adults in the sin bin

The scene: a weekend soccer pitch, Australian suburbia. Two teams of primary school kids and a dad on the sidelines, letting rip with a foul-mouthed tirade at the ref. Children within earshot – on the field, among the spectators.

I've seen it and cringed, seen the shock of the kids confronted by it. The diminishing little episodes feel sourly adult, the aggro so removed from what the kids are there to actually do: have fun, be with mates, learn some skills. Recently, Hawthorn coach Alastair Clarkson swore at a 19-year-old official during his son's under-nine match; Clarkson, who'd been acting as a runner, was ordered to leave the field. Geelong goal umpire Tiffany Farrow, 15, has had rocks thrown at her in senior games but says junior matches are worse: 'I've found [parents] the worst spectators to have because they always think their son is right, or that I'm not because [their son] missed a goal.'

There are mates who'll say yours truly is the person least

qualified to write about this – as, er, the ultimate anti-spectator. Yes, the one who fled these fair shores in terror as the world's most non-sporty Australian. Ditto the chap. Yet somehow we've bred two soccer-obsessed mini chaps who live, breathe and dream the beautiful game. Isn't nature wonderful? Their parents: the pathetic lot who use the weekly footy match to catch up on blissful slabs of reading. Mates will swear blind the head's never been raised from the iPad; in fact a friend nudges me with 'look up, Mum' at crucial moments (for this, eternal gratitude).

But enough games have been witnessed over the years to wonder at the heartbreaking, exhilarating psychodrama of it all. Favourite player: the little goalie, for sheer courage in volunteering for that thankless task. Favourite match time: those last five minutes when everything's charged; desperate, tiny hearts bursting as they try to sway the game, retrieve the honour. Favourite mum moment of awe: the seasons when they've endured crushingly long losing streaks, yet every week they've strapped on their shinpads, bursting with hope, anticipation, the sheer moving love of the game. Plunging eagerly back into the fray, week after week, *this* time, maybe ...

A lot's been written recently about why continental Europe's producing better teams than England (and Australia, of course). Portuguese football manager Jose Mourinho: 'In England you teach your kids to win. In Portugal and Spain they teach their kids how to play football.' I can vouch for that. A group of young Brazilian men sometimes end up on our local beach at twilight, soccer ball in tow. It's beautiful to watch (all right, girls, beautiful in many ways to watch). But they're playing, above all, generously passing the ball; twisting, leaping, diving; it's almost balletic. The local kids join in; everyone has a blast. 'We play like this on the streets, it's life, how we were raised,' explained one. Albert Capellas, formerly FC Barcelona's youth coordinator, said: 'It's very important for us that the boys have respect for others. They have to be good people, like gentlemen.' That spirit feels a world away from the parents venting their immature rage every weekend across Australia.

We're all outraged now, about so much. The hurt, the affront is everywhere and don't we bleat it, furiously? The modern world feels like a tinderbox of indignation, fuelled by a sense of entitlement, an erosion of civility, a simmering anger. Adults are often far worse than the kids. I'm guilty. Beeping the horn when driving, groaning at cyclists, swearing. And from the back of the car? Stunned silence. From kids who are better than me. Who've had it drummed into them that they're not allowed to cuss. If I'm feeling big enough I'll apologise, but the car invariably feels grubbied, soured, in those telling silences. I'm not proud of my flashes of childish outrage. Are you?

(Originally published in the *Australian Weekend Magazine*, 25 August 2012)

Paternally grateful

Is there a word for it? I can't think of one. The label 'maternal' is fenced off by women, exclusively, proudly; 'paternal' – well, feminism has stained its meaning, it's veered into something hegemonic, domineering, controlling, hardened, a word a lot of females flinch from by instinct.

But how to describe what I see all around me, in boys as well as men? It requires a very particular modern word but I don't know it. What is it I'm trying to describe?

The sight of young boys in a school playground – nine, ten, 11 – delightedly, confidently passing around a baby like a pass-the-parcel; boys having competitions to get the child laughing; helping him with his first galumphing, wobbling steps. There's such an open, kind, giggly tenderness in them; something, dare I say, deeply maternal – even more so than the girls. But of course it's not described like that. I see it in my father, who wants to steal the kids whenever he visits; showers them with presents, cuddles, the gift of his attention, blows raspberries on tiny tummies, disentangles them from fishing rods; 'go away, Mum, they're mine now'. I see it in the chap, making three lots of school lunches every weeknight no matter how big a workday he's had, getting up at dawn every weekend to get to an obscure footy pitch, camping out at his sons' school this Father's Day weekend despite an extreme aversion to tents, sleeping bags and the lack of good coffee anywhere in sight. The man who held each one of his children in the first hour of their lives and wept, held them strong and possessive and proud yet with infinite gentleness. And as I witnessed it, every time, I thought this is an emotion as powerful, magnificent, pure, as anything a woman can lay claim to.

But what is the word that encapsulates all this? That distinctly modern, easy, masculine tenderness towards a young child. A great liberation of feminism is that men are allowed to be so much more in touch with their feminine side, and when we women discern the confidence of this graceful way of being we celebrate it. There's something deeply satisfying to it, in a biological sense.

But then this: the collective, reactive flinch at a lone male, in public, with children. It was recently reported that, in May, Virgin Australia removed Sydney fireman Johnny McGirr from his seat because he was sitting next to two unaccompanied boys. Mr McGirr: '[The attitude of the airline] is "we respect you but as soon as you board a Virgin airline you are a potential paedophile", and that strips away all the good that any male does regardless of his standing in society, his profession or his moral attitudes.' A new soft play centre in England's Birmingham has declared that fathers and boys over nine are not welcome. My own children's nursery in London once hired a male teacher; the result, a flurry of horror and panic among some parents and a destructive, divisive campaign to have him turfed out.

It's such a shame, all this. Because I look at those boys in their schoolground playing so joyfully with a baby and think what wonderful fathers they'll all make, whatever their sexual orientation in adulthood. Men of the new world indeed. This paranoid suspicion of the male in public, with kids, feels like a betrayal of the easy, fluid innocence of our young men. We're in a world that doesn't celebrate the word I'm looking for, whatever it is. In 'A Small Journal' American poet Anne Sexton wrote: 'It doesn't matter who my father was; it matters who I remember he was.' The memories of my own father involve tenderness and cherishing and a fierce love of the child, qualities that do not reduce his masculinity – but enhance it. So Happy Father's Day, to all of you out there. And thank you. A lot of us women notice what you do and are deeply moved by it.

We just don't say it enough.

(Originally published in the *Australian Weekend Magazine*, 1 September 2012)

Mind your language

During that recent, unedifying scandal involving the UK's Barclays Bank and the fixing of Libor interest rates, former chief executive Bob Diamond's daughter, Nell, allegedly tweeted about two senior government figures: 'George Osborne and Ed Miliband you can go ahead and HMD.' Cue a torrent of internet chatter about what on Earth she meant. 'Hold my dick,' actually. Charming.

And from a woman raised in the lap of luxury, educated at one of London's finest girls' schools and then one of America's most prestigious universities. Ah, the gobby young female of today with the world at her feet, the smorgasbord of social media spread before her.

The temptation to be so bolshy, loud, fast, raucous – and crude. (And so reduced by one unthinking tweet – Ms Diamond has since left her job as an analyst at Deutsche Bank.) It got me thinking about those particularly female sayings thrown over back fences all over Australia, sayings fast disappearing from our discourse. Those pithy little put-downs from our grandmothers, mothers, neighbours, aunts that are rapidly being leached from the lexicon. Insulting, yes, but often deliciously funny, spot on … and never ugly. 'She's as plain as a Sao biscuit.' 'He was behind the door when the looks were handed out.' 'He was such a busybody he wanted to know the ins and outs of a magpie's backside.' 'Not enough brains to give himself a headache.'

'She was so annoyed she came down the path with her legs plaited.' 'He had a tongue so sharp it could cut a hedge.' And in celebration of a particularly gorgeous baby: 'He's off the Christmas tree, that one' (i.e., a bauble). Can't you just picture the Hills Hoist, the rollers in the hair, the quilted dressing gown? It's relatively easy to find the more masculine Aussie sayings, often involving body parts and functions and intense crudity, but these female ones are harder to come by. You have to ask, have to find the women who still remember them, still use them. The muscularity of our language! Bingle, tingle, shonky and squizz, bludger and wowser, clobber and togs. Oh, don't get me started.

When I lived in Alice, the local Aboriginal phrases took on a whole new level of deliciousness: 'waterbeds' for the cops, because they went up and down, up and down the mall. 'Lady in a boat' for grog, named after the Coolabah cask that had the woman in her white dress sitting in a boat.

And 'whackfellas': non-Aboriginal persons who espouse an extremely earnest connection to the spirituality of Aboriginal people – and who may or may not wear dreadlocks and/or play a didjeridoo – but whose interest is really only superficial (i.e., they're all for land rights but have little understanding of the political nuances behind it all). Just glorious.

I'm a regular magpie in terms of fabulously colourful local words. Scotland's another treasure trove for the mellifluous gorgeousness of its language. 'Simmer dim', from the Shetland Isles: that time of no-darkness on a summer's night, the twilight loveliness around midnight that never deepens into a proper black. Smirr: a mist-like precipitation, a soft rain. Gurly: rough or boisterous. Galoot: idiot. Blootered: extremely drunk. Crabit: grumpy.

Then there's London street slang. Blud, meaning brother or sister or mate. Garms: clothing. Lush: good-looking. Wifey: girlfriend. Wicked: cool, but then so is sick. And everything bad is rubbish.

So what are the young Aussies of today bestowing upon our language? The word du jour in these parts: 'owned'. As in 'you're owned, Mum', as in 'got the better of' (and it's happening far too much for my liking at the moment). So, dear reader, any phrases from times past that I can throw back at the little buggers are most welcome. Because many, so many, are just too delicious to have them disappear on us.

(Originally published in the *Australian Weekend Magazine*, 8 September 2012)

Don't take it lying down

How will history record the media's performance during this period of national fractiousness, tetchiness, affront? Courageous, perhaps? Fair-minded? Rigorous?

And this, of course, at a momentous juncture in the profession's history, when traditional forms of media are fighting for survival. We need ennobling stories here. Television executive Elisabeth Murdoch recently told industry bods that every company needs a 'set of values based on an explicit statement of purpose'; that the absence of a 'moral language' could be calamitous. It was a clarion call for responsibility, compassion, vision. She concluded her MacTaggart lecture with: 'Tell great stories, inspire audiences and contribute to a sense of community.'

Great stories. I've been thinking about that recently in terms of our PM. The Meryl Streep biopic of Margaret Thatcher was a clear if dramatically oversimplified narrative of a life robustly lived, yet we find it hard to grasp who Julia Gillard really is. It's difficult to glean a moving story arc because she rarely shows us her true self: she's so careful, cautious, so damned lawyerly about saying the right thing. But then there are those arresting moments when the real Julia blazes through. Answering questions about the Slater & Gordon years – an exhaustive, witty, eloquent chastening. Remarking on Tony Abbott's party room comments: 'Recently, I got the best compliment of my lifetime from an unexpected quarter, when it was said about me that "Gillard will not lay down and die".'

To which I thought, 'Damn right.' A stirring riposte for any woman who's ever been belittled, mocked, ignored. And if there's one thing we women have become very good at, it's enduring. Through continual putdowns, through bad sex, through being told we're not funny, can't drive, are dumb. That's why I'm willing Lara Bingle to keep going as much as I'm willing Julia Gillard to. Because these women won't lie down and die, as much as some people want them to. Don't let the mockers win, I say – don't disappear, be silent, submissive – it's what these people want. Females in their 'rightful place'.

All this at a time when women have never been more empowered in terms of education, careers, leadership. Alongside it, a disturbing swell of misogyny. Sydney's Anglican Church requesting women pledge to 'submit' in marriage vows. British PM David Cameron saying, 'Calm down, dear,' to a female politician. Karl Lagerfeld labelling the singer Adele 'too fat' and taking umbrage at Pippa Middleton's face: 'She should only show her back.' Our own female basketballers flying premium economy to the Olympics but their male counterparts flying business class.

We don't want favourable treatment, we want fair treatment. A lot of the media seem curiously unwilling to scrutinise both leaders to an equal extent. But there was a shift in consciousness when Leigh Sales recently interviewed Tony Abbott on the *7.30 Report*. It felt like a woman who'd had enough; a woman who courageously wanted to inject a little equality into the national debate; to be as hard on Abbott as she would ever be on Gillard. For this she was labelled 'a cow' by Liberal strategist Grahame Morris.

Would that our banks – in terms of interest rates and obscene profit margins – be put under as much scrutiny and pressure. But we all know that's not going to happen. Yet with these flashes of the real Julia we're starting to see the narrative that may make a great biopic. I fear, though, she'll be a historical anomaly; it'll be a long time before we ever see another female PM. Look at Britain since Thatcher – no woman's got close. It's just too risky, divisive, fraught. For my daughter's generation, and generations beyond it, this breaks my heart.

(Originally published in the *Weekend Australian Magazine*, 15 September 2012)

Time out!

Don't make it too easy for them. I contemplated that little truism following a despairing email from a father attempting some down-time with his wife, in their room, on a Saturday night.

'Da-ad,' came the cry from outside. A child barged in. As they do.

'Why have we allowed our kids to consider us always accessible?' he wrote. 'Growing up I knew that once my parents' door was closed, they were off-limits. Are we not instilling enough respect now for other people's time and space alone?'

Mate, I'm with you. Contemplated your frustration as I tried showering in peace this morning but was constantly interrupted by shouts of 'Mum, where's my uniform?' 'Can you pour my cereal?' 'Did you organise the playdate?' accompanied by a symphony of toddler bangs on the door. It made me think of those reader tales of a peculiarly modern parental despair: going to the carwash just to read, because it's the one place where the baby's silent and contained; sitting *in* the playpen to escape while the toddlers rampage outside. Oh yes, there's a whole generation of parents desperate to flee the kids, just now and then; to glean some precious drops of replenishing 'me time' in the great mad whoosh of our lives.

How has the power balance shifted so dramatically in the parent/child dynamic? I'm often informed by my boys that I'm pwned – 'owned' in internet speak, got the better of – yet saying something like that to an adult, when I was a kid, would have been the height of insolence. There's a cheeky, jostling camaraderie now but yours truly is always the fall guy in it: the embarrassing one who needs teaching in the ways of this world. According to psychology professors Jean Twenge and W. Keith Campbell: 'Parents want their kids' approval [now], a reversal of the past ideal of children striving for their parents' approval.'

Modern children seem so entitled, confident, wilful, with scant little respect for adult boundaries. Dare I say, the fault lies in the parenting. I'm not sure why we feel the path to success lies in micromanaging our children's lives, but I've fallen into that trap along with just about every parent I know. We do so ridiculously much for them: intervene, meddle, hover. Yet I know in my bones that the ignored child is the more self-sufficient child, possibly the more successful child (just look at Churchill's childhood of magnificently nonchalant parental neglect – they never made it easy for him).

We aim for calm, centred, self-sufficient kids – yet seem lost how to nurture those qualities. Once it was parents yelling, 'Skedaddle, and don't appear 'til the street lights switch on'; now we're too scared to let them meander to the corner shop in case they're kidnapped, run over, lost. Yet they'll never become adults if we don't let them attempt some responsibility (thanks, Seth Rogen and the rest of you, I see the future and it scares me: kidults, still, at 40).

This attitude's leaching into the adult world – in outbursts of rage on the road, trolling on social media, bullying on the airwaves. What is it, above all? Juvenile. A society that's not letting its youngest mature naturally into adults with all the decorum, self-possession and restraint that's meant to entail. Just writing this column makes me all hot and bothered. Several kids in this house were recently naughty and a new punishment was instituted: the Foxtel card was confiscated. For a week. Cue howls of outrage.

Reader, it worked. After the initial protests a soldering calm settled on the house, a vast blanket of peace. The kids retreated to rooms, were bored but found their way into reading, drawing, dreaming. It felt wondrous and rare and old-fashioned; felt like our world exhaled into order. But soon, I know, we'll slip back. We're modern parents, after all.

(Originally published in the *Australian Weekend Magazine*, 22 September 2012)

My four-legged friend

Oh you beautiful thing you. Peeping out from behind a tree, abandoned, shy, out of place in this dank pocket of the local reserve. I can see the bones of you: you're a beauty under all that neglect. Over several days you're watched. No one else is interested. In the end you're hauled home in a mighty, dragging effort. Goodness knows what to do with you but you can't be left to an unappreciated fate ...

You're an old squatter's chair. Just the frame. An original. With flaps swivelling out from under the arms to become leg rests, perfectly suited for the Aussie bush verandah after a hard day's yakka.

Our first ones were made from bullock yokes slung with flour sacks. My beauty's made of ironbark bleached to a tough silver grey, legs as shapely as a Victorian woman's, the timber extensions held in place by wide, pleasing buttons.

I've rescued the bones of you but how to flesh you out? No upholsterer's enthused and so you sit abandoned in the backyard through rain and wind and sun. Your time will come.

You're a celebration of simplicity. I'm a sucker for that. There are many vices; the worst – akrasia – is a lack of self-control. The chap will attest it's most evident on weekends when he hears, nonchalantly, 'I'm just going outside and may be some time,' and cringes, for the boot's likely to come back filled with junk shop accumulations. Francis Bacon spoke of 'the mystery of appearance', and for me, often, it's the little heart-lift when a Depression-era chest of drawers made out of kerosene tins is spied, a sun-bleached dresser with thick convict nails, a sieve the size of a truck's wheel. Simple, wondrous, ingenious things that speak of the muscularity and functionality of Australia's past; people who made do, fashioning things out of nothing with vigour and cunning and humour.

I've never liked Le Corbusier's maxim, 'A house is a machine for living in'; for me a house is a place for mooring in, a sanctuary of stillness amid the great gallop of life; a place that gladdens your heart as you step across the threshold; that calms you, unclenches you, releases you into a space where you can be your true self. Simplicity is key, obfuscation loathed. We were bequeathed an electronic gate for the carport; it's as skittish as a thoroughbred, temperamental, precious, constantly chucking sickies. In the end we begged the manufacturers for the simplicity of a key so we could just do the darned thing manually. Bliss.

Steve Jobs knew simplicity's potency: 'Simple can be harder than complex,' he said. 'You have to work hard to get your thinking clean to make it simple. But it's worth it in the end because once you get there, you can move mountains.' Don't get me started on our complicated tangle of TV, Foxtel box and Wii. Do you think I can get any of it started? Thank God for kids. It reminds me of hotel rooms that seem designed to vex you. Why do they not understand the beauty of simplicity? Does the front desk really have to be rung to unplug the bath or turn off lights?

Back to my squatter's chair. Two sturdy gym mats from World War I are stumbled across. A quickening; these will do. Plus some rolls of vintage hessian webbing. What follows: an absorbing, soldering afternoon with a staple gun. I'm sitting in the chair now, writing, legs up and crossed, the laptop on a plank across the arm rests. It's obscenely comfortable, my little aerie in the living room from where the whole jumbly spread of kids, homework, kitchen and backyard can be surveyed. The thinking is clean here; minutes, hours, can pass in a golden gaze of nothing and everything. The past presses close: sun and sweat and aching bodies unfurling, falling asleep in the long evening light, a hat over a face after a hard day in the saddle checking fences, calving. A story idea is sparked ...

(Originally published in the *Weekend Australian Magazine*, 29 September 2012)

A hard day's night

Imagine that walloping feeling of jetlag, day after day. Being zippily, speedily, glarily awake, then dragged down into sleep in a way that's beyond your control; your body insisting you lie down, urgently, compelling you to shut your eyes no matter what needs to be done. You're held hostage by the torments of sleep – the craving for it, the lack of it. Imagine setting your clock for 3am, then tossing and turning with growing panic as the minutes tick by towards the shrill of the alarm; you can't fall into slumber no matter what. It's 2am. Still not asleep. Pillow punched in frustration. Finally, finally, you fall ... then the alarm blares and your heart pounds as you drag yourself up in the thick velvety darkness of everyone else asleep. You think, 'I cannot do this, cannot get up.' But the adrenalin kicks in ...

Welcome to the world of the shift worker. Australian sleep research scientist Dr Carmel Harrington says it's a work regime that throws up all sorts of health issues, and they need addressing. Her book, *The Sleep Diet*, details the punishing effects of it: increased incidences of obesity, cardiovascular disease, breast and prostate cancers, diabetes and depression. The problem is the jarring disruption to naturally occurring body rhythms. The effects can feel obscene, driving you to irrationality, altering your personality.

I did 4am starts at the Sydney ABC newsroom and overnights at the BBC World Service in London – never got used to either. It was women I observed the most: some stopped menstruating, others struggled to conceive or miscarried, others needed medication for depression. Says Harrington: 'It's amazing that so many people who work shifts suffer these consequences and so often are unaware that it's due to the hours they work.' She says the incidences of breast cancer are 60 per cent higher in women working nights (starting after 7pm), most likely because of the improper production of melatonin – the hormone produced in the dark hours. Your body feels like it's never, quite, catching up. Imagine finishing your working day at 7am and emerging into the mewly London light just as the great stream of people are heading into the metropolis, into the opposite world to you. The right one. And my night-shift pattern was one week on, two off (as in one week of nights, two weeks of days), so I never adjusted to a steady rhythm.

My father worked shifts for 60 years, on and off; he's just come off a coal mine walking 13 km a night doing safety checks. He says it's this modern regime of altering shift patterns that has the most adverse effects. 'In the old days it was five days of eight-hour night shifts, Monday to Friday,' he says. 'So your sleep pattern was repetitive. It didn't knock you around too much; you'd recover on the weekend. But with the introduction of massive mines in remote places there are all different rosters. Seven on, seven off is the most popular.' He's worked 28 on, 14 off in Indonesia, and has seen blokes who work in different mines on their days off. 'It's a recipe for disaster. Tiredness is endemic, you're under stress, isolated, bored – it makes the workers difficult to control. They're stroppy; just not as productive now. They're too brain dead.' Then they have to get themselves home.

Yesterday I spoke to my grandmother's doctor – Nan's 99, in hospital. I'd caught the medico at the end of his night shift, about to set off on a 90-minute drive home. 'Be careful,' I said softly, because I know what it's like to navigate your way after a gruelling shift. Dad, once, ended up with his car in the bush – he'd fallen asleep at the wheel. Anyone who doesn't have to do shift work – who's not held hostage by the tyranny of the alarm clock in the early hours, or worse, at four in the afternoon – should be grateful. It's a bloody hard existence. Shift workers of Australia, I salute you.

(Originally published in the *Weekend Australian Magazine*, 13 October 2012)

A fine vintage

'For me, there are only two kinds of women – goddesses and doormats.' Ah, the wisdom of Picasso, and it's well documented he liked them submissive; if they weren't that at the start of a relationship he'd try to crack them with his cruelty. I thought of this at a gathering of Australian women earlier this year for *InStyle* magazine; not a doormat among them. 'I want to be you when I grow up,' declared MC Jessica Rowe to an older woman among the crowd; cue a stirring of concurrence, a collective girl-crush. The recipient? Jana Wendt. And this with a posse of youthful gorgeousness in the mix – the Mirandas Kerr and Otto, Asher Keddie, Megan Washington. But what was extraordinary: the women who'd been around the block a few times, yet could still rock a black velvet sheath, were getting the lion's share of the adulation. Middle-aged chicks who were the embodiment of confidence, intelligence, poise, contentment and sheer damned hotness; women completely comfortable in their skin.

The delight was roguish through me at this appreciation of the older female. It felt like the future, *our* future. No one was there because of who they'd slept with or married; these were women who'd done it, gloriously, for themselves – and it seemed like a seismic shift in how we view this older demographic.

These quietly powerful chicks in their 50s and 60s are the vanguard of the future feminisation of the planet; confident, educated, articulate, feminine women. It's a potent mix. They feel neither old nor irrelevant nor invisible.

All this as I career towards the wintry side of the mid-40s. But it's not that at all! OK, it feels like there are more eyelids than there used to be and the grey hairs are shooting most unbecomingly heavenward as if they're already craning for the light, but I don't see these as years of decline, at all. They're about burgeoning freedom and power. You see my speciality, once, was niceness, acquiesce, the big yes, until I was worn thin from it. Now I've found the power of 'no'. Am no longer cowed by what people think; still buy Topshop shoes alongside the teenagers, still sneak a banana Paddle Pop now and then, still dance up a storm to James singing 'Laid' on the iPod. Apparently 50th birthdays are much more fun than 40ths – because you're much lighter, relaxed. There's less angst about what you haven't achieved yet; the intensity of the baby years, for many, has passed and you no longer feel shunted aside from your own life. You've reclaimed it, joyously; you're at peace.

As for those men with their dramatically younger women beside them: they don't look empowered anymore, they look sad. He may think it's a sign of his virility, we see it as a sign of insecurity. The real power, mate, is having the confidence to exist comfortably alongside the voice, brains and beauty of one of these lionesses of the new era; not to be threatened but enhanced by them.

Earlier this year I saw Jane Birkin on stage. As she appeared you could feel the collective sigh from women across the audience – we wanted to be her. She was in loose black pants and blazer and what looked like a lover's white shirt. As the evening wore on the jacket was discarded and the shirt loosened, revealing a peek of the coolest bra: pale with thick black piping. This was a 65-year-old who looked liked she loved laughing in bed – still. She was an appreciator; chatting infectiously about Serge Gainsbourg and love and grandkids, her enthusiasm ardent, giggly, youthful. What a life she's led and she zings with it; it's a welling of experience and endurance and warmth and grace. You're our future, I thought, a future way of being; you're blazing the path, girl. Alongside Jana and Quentin and Michelle. Goddesses, the lot of you.

(Originally published in the *Weekend Australian Magazine*, 6 October 2012)

Essays

Anonymity

Why did I do it?

Behold a cautionary tale of writing, refuges, and worlds to be free in.

Once upon a time I had a brilliant idea. Well, it seemed like it at the time. The plan was simple: to write a novel that was an examination of marriage with a forensic, unsparing eye. But book writing has always been a process of gradual disappointment for me; the grand ambition of each project contracting over time as I realise that what is emerging on the page wasn't, quite, what had been envisaged at the outset. To be blunt: my novels slip away in the process of creation, become something else. And so I'd just try again, and again, to get it right; that was the rhythm of my novel-writing and each subsequent book. Early on, this tetchy new book – my fourth – about sex and marriage was not going to plan. I had a title, *The Bride Stripped Bare,* and not much else. The disappointment was gathering force heart-sinkingly soon into the process. Six months in, in fact. The story just wouldn't lift off. The prose was resistant, leaden. Trying to write it was like wading thigh high through a river rushing towards me. Definitely not a good situation to be in with a newborn baby by my side, my first, and another little one on the way (the lesson here: do not believe those who tell you it is impossible to conceive while breastfeeding).

Then one day, in the thick of new motherhood, I chanced upon Virginia Woolf's *A Room of One's Own*. It was the type of book I hadn't read for a while, drowning as I was under my sea of baby-manuals, and I seized that clear, sharply intelligent prose; remembering a woman I was who devoured books like this once. Woolf described anonymity as a 'refuge' for women writers. 'For most of history, Anonymous was a woman.' And with that simple sentence, my recalcitrant novel was unlocked.

It was as if a lightbulb was suddenly switched on in a room of sickly light. My name would be removed from the project. Simple. I'd write with brutal candour about a women's secret life – and brilliantly, no one would be hurt in the process. Myself, of course, but also those closest to me in that precious little coracle of early parenthood we were floating in then, that tiny boat of nappies and naptimes and leaky breasts and wonder, endless wonder, that contained just my husband and our child and our new one soon to join us. Because I knew that if was going to write something with eviscerating honesty there would be reverberations years down the track, for all of us. People have always confused my fiction with autobiography; I've always had readers assume it was people close to me who were in my books, and judging them as well as myself. I was seized up by a fear of that; that they would mistake fiction for fact. And as I'd struggled to make that sodden first draft work I'd felt clogged up with caution – afraid of too much honesty, of showing too much vulnerability, and afraid of hurting people close to me.

The door was flung open, gleefully, when anonymity presented itself. 'The world was made to be free in. Give up on all other worlds except the one to which you belong,' the poet David Whyte wrote. Oh yes. *The Bride Stripped Bare* was brewed in a blazing little world far removed from any other. It shone with light, and truth, and power; a deep and thrilling sense of satisfaction amid all the exhaustion and uncertainty of new parenthood. It was my one certainty, my anchor. I didn't want publishers breathing down my neck. Didn't tell them about it. My previous book, *Lovesong*, had had its ending compromised in the rush to meet a contractual deadline and I never wanted to get into that situation again. *Bride* freed me again, as a writer. If this book wasn't sold when completed it would be slipped into a bottom drawer and that would be the end of it, it would be 'one that didn't work'. No one was expecting it. Agents and publishers had written me off into babyland for several years at least, perhaps longer. In their eyes I'd disappeared.

Gloriously. Mischievously. Writing became fun again, exhilarating.

Gabriel Garcia Marquez said every person has three lives: a public life, which is known to everyone in the spheres we move in; a private life, which perhaps just a partner or close family member knows; and a secret life. That was the one I was fascinated by. Who dares to presume they know anyone else's secret life? I wanted to write about a woman's secret world – any woman's; if you like, *every* woman's. Wanted to write about the raw underbelly of a woman's thinking in all its complexity, all its shocking ugliness as well as its beauty. It could only be done with the gift of anonymity, the egoless existence that liberates you from what people think, frees from the indignant eye of public opinion, from judgment. And some of this book would be eviscerating.

Why not just go for it? Say whatever I wanted to, all those things I'd been thinking, feeling, for years but had never had the courage to voice. Not to girlfriends, and certainly not to partners. The whole idea of it fitted snugly into that egoless existence of early parenthood, when all my wants/needs/ desires are subsumed by someone else. Basically, at that point in my life, I just didn't care a jot about my name on a book, because I had bigger things filling up my days. And the glary business of selling my work – emotionally investing in its precarious journey into the world – was just too swamping to think about within the thick of the babymoon. I write within what feels like the glow of candlelight, a world that's still and quiet and vividly alone, but selling a book, as the author, is like a sudden blast of fluorescent light. I'm a writer who doesn't enjoy that side of the business; in fact, gets a knot of agitation at the thought of it. Anonymity was my rescue.

The words came strong. Fast. I wrote with the arrogance and innocence of my first novel, *Shiver*. I'd not had that sense of a quickening, a rightness, as I laboured through the second and third novels, weighed down not only by publisher and reader expectations but my own. As I was writing *Bride* I was high on hormones, flushed with a sense of womanly invincibility. It felt easy. This manuscript would be the child conceived and carried then let go of at the orphanage gate, now and then checked on from afar. The perfect plan. For after all, I had other children – real children – cramming every corner of my life. I wrote with an unflinching veracity. Wrote of sex that was bursting with light and life; all the magic and messiness of life as we know it. It wasn't porn in any way, the opposite of it in fact. It was a brutally honest take on sex, from a woman's perspective. (Porn – urgh. When I think of that I think of something bleak, mechanical, unreal, ugly – and with an utter absence of tenderness.) I wanted a book driven by love and truth; a book where women would respond, 'Oh, that's me!' and where men would respond, 'Oh my goodness, did my partner write this?'

Having 'By Anonymous' bold on the cover felt crucial to that sense of enchantment, cheekiness, artifice, honesty. Removing the author's name meant the book carried with it a shock of universality. This could be anyone's story. Not just 'so and so's opinion' but anyone's, everyone's. It felt audacious and authentic and absolutely right.

For after all it's hard, in a relationship, to be completely honest, to show your partner your secret self. Vita Sackville-West described herself as an iceberg, said that her husband could only see what was above the water's surface and that he had no idea of the huge mass below. She speculated it was the reason their marriage worked. What relationship can survive the shock of absolute candour?

For me, brewing my little secret during baby naptimes, the jolt of *Bride* would lie in the protagonist's very ordinariness. She'd be the woman you don't give a second glance to as she walks down an aisle in the supermarket or waits patiently at the school gate; the woman who's completely disappeared into her role as 'the little wife'.

I, too, had found it difficult to be completely sexually honest in the past, and was fascinated by the capitulations and silences that can stain a relationship – but also knit it together. Why is it still so hard for some women, basking in the glow of so many feminist advances, to be more candid about sex? To say such simple things to our sexual partners as, 'No, I didn't have an orgasm,' or 'I don't like this,' or 'Sometimes I find it monotonous when you make love to me,' or 'Sometimes it hurts.' Why are so many women still so subservient to their partner's pleasure at the expense of their own? Because we don't want men to turn away from us, perhaps. Because we want our partners to think we're someone else. Because sometimes we're willing to put up with a lot: to snare a relationship, to keep it steady, to have children.

The aim was to be as merciless in print as a Chuck Close painting or a Ron Mueck sculpture – but as far as I know, those artists do not often turn their extremely critical eye upon themselves. Now I know why. I'm not someone who's completely relaxed about nudity; I've never been comfortable in a bikini. And like many women in a swimsuit, I'm afraid of revealing too much. But when the idea of anonymity came to me, everything clicked. I was suddenly like a woman on a foreign beach who's confident she doesn't know a soul and parades her body loudly and joyously without worrying what anyone thinks of her. A lot of us can't face the thought of people seeing us as we really are – for it means losing control of the public persona we've so carefully set up and maintained. And we never get closer to the truth of our dark, vulnerable, messy selves than with sex. Perhaps that's why the prospect of being unmasked as the author of this book was so very difficult to bear. Perhaps if I was alone, without family around me who I deeply cared about, it would have been easier. Another reason for the anonymity was that it came from a deep love, a deep sense of compassion – I wanted to protect so much.

Anonymity also meant I wasn't afraid of *Bride* failing. It seemed such a strange hybrid of novel, memoir, treatise and sex manual and I wasn't sure if people would 'get' it. I'd lost my professional confidence. My brain just didn't work in the way it used to. The previous novel had gone to sixty drafts over several intensive years and I just didn't have the stamina, the mental elasticity, to work that way again, or to worry over whether it worked.

Bride is also a response to another anonymous text: a mysterious 17th-century document known as *WoEman's Worth*. Its tone is boldly sexual, its honesty shocking and its authorship disputed. Germaine Greer believes it was written by a man close to his mother; others say it was by an anonymous housewife. I choose to believe the latter and loved the idea of a 21st-century housewife also writing a secret book under the nose of her husband. Saying all those things she might think but never say – even in this sexually liberated day and age. I loved the boldly subversive, almost cheeky tone of the 17th-century text – and recognised it. The author could only have written these charged, highly subversive sexual declarations in secret. I wanted to respond to the author, say: 'Hey, it's 400 years later and women have come a long way, but actually, not so far in some matters.' I was intrigued that this 17th-century writer seemed to have more confidence, sexually, than a Western woman in the 21st century who's lived through several decades of feminist advances.

So there I had it. A vivid little manuscript with 'By Anonymous' on its front page. It was sent off, heart in mouth, to my literary agent in London. Because he of course knew it was really me, knew what type of a woman and writer I was –

and I didn't want to be associated with this kind of book. His response? Silence. For weeks. Agony. Of course, I reasoned, it was all just too damned vulgar, crude, embarrassing – and this man almost 60 cannot bear to face me. Great. I've lost an agent now as well as my writing confidence and possibly my career. Then, after several excruciatingly long weeks, the phone rang. The manuscript had been sitting on his 'pile' that he hadn't got around to amid all the busyness. But a girlfriend of his son had picked it up the past weekend, read it, and said 'I think you should take a look at this ...'

He did. He called instantly. The manuscript went to the Frankfurt Book Fair. At that point only he and three people in the UK publisher's office knew of the book's authorship, as well as several trusted writer friends and my husband. I was feeling good, my agent was excited and I trusted his judgment implicitly; we had a 'goer' on our hands. Just after the Fair I read a newspaper article at a London bus stop. It said an anonymous book had caused a sensation in Frankfurt. In normal circumstances this news would be the cause of much exhilaration in an author. Yet my heart beat faster in panic. For you see, the article was brimming with speculation about who the mystery author could be. Disgruntled wife of a former Booker winner? Suburban housewife? Man? It was a call to arms to track down the writer's identity. As a former journalist, I knew it would only be a matter of time. My heart sank.

It took just a week. On a night my husband and I will never forget, we were subjected to the terrier-like force of Fleet

Street's finest: incessant phone calls, door-thumping until almost midnight, babies waking and screaming in terror. The reporter who broke the story said the writing style pointed to one author in particular. This was of some comfort, for I've always aimed for a distinctive voice as a writer. The reporter went on to say the author's identity was confirmed by a senior figure in the British publishing industry. This was of no comfort. Suddenly, trusted friends and business associates became evil, Machiavellian blabbermouths. Felt besieged. Trusting no one, suspecting everyone – publishers, my agent's office – until I eventually thought: oh Lordy, it was probably someone pissed at a cocktail party. And most likely one of my writer mates. 'The fewer writers you know the better,' the writer Maeve Brennan cautioned once, 'and if you're working on anything, don't tell them.'

I'll never be able to face the journalist who broke the story. That feeling, back then, was of one huge flinch. I'd lost control of my book, and my brand as a writer. My little baby was suddenly everybody else's and I didn't like it one bit. No one's ever given a hint of how it happened. I still don't know who 'shopped' me. Spent several years afterwards trying to work out who'd done it. A phone hacker, some have since suggested, for after all it was rife among newspapers in London at the time.

The problem, as a writer, was that I was outed before the book had been edited. I went back to my editor, the gracious but steely Courtney Hodell, armed with a red pen. 'I'm deleting so much,' I declared, 'and I know exactly which bits.' Because I was unable to face my name being attached to so many of the rawer passages in the book. 'Don't,' she pleaded. Why? 'Because all those passages are the excruciatingly honest ones, the things that readers will connect with the most.' I couldn't bear it. It wasn't the way I wanted my career to veer. We argued. There were tears. She won. In hindsight, she was right. But I couldn't see it then; still trying to protect so many small kingdoms, still unable to emerge from the world I'd been made free in. I just didn't want to embrace any other brutal, mocking, indignant, cynical world, didn't want to publicly own this book.

I felt, above all, hugely naïve. On the day of the book's publication in Britain my publisher insisted on a celebratory lunch. OK, I said, OK, even though I didn't particularly feel like one – wasn't sure the situation actually called for celebration. But for a writer it's not a politic thing to refuse a publisher's lunch – especially if your agent and publicist have also been invited – so I dressed to the nines and ordered a taxi to take me to a very smart restaurant indeed. This was an occasion, after all. And I'd never been to this restaurant. It's a fabulously expensive one, and I'm a writer.

The taxi driver picked me up precisely when he'd been ordered and traffic was flowing smoothly, I'd arrive on time, all was going well. But about 10 minutes from our destination I started weeping. Couldn't stop. My gentle Afghani driver kept on turning in alarm, asking if I was alright, wanting to take me home. 'I'll be fine,' I said, wiping tears furiously from my cheeks. I asked to be dropped off around the corner from the restaurant. The taxi driver didn't want to let me out into the world, he was being extremely fatherly; I insisted. But as I waved goodbye to this kindly man, smiling a tight smile, the dam burst. He disappeared into the distance and the tears became great keening howls and there I was, on the day of *The Bride Stripped Bare*'s publication, wandering the streets of London's Fitzrovia as if I'd just suffered the most terrible bereavement. I must say this strange episode restored my faith in humanity, for many huge-hearted people came up and asked if they could get me a glass of water, if I wanted to sit down, rest, use their mobile phone. What I couldn't tell any of them was that I had written an excruciatingly honest account of sex, anonymously, and had been found out. And on this auspicious day it was, well, just too much to bear.

Stress rushed into my world in a greedy, ruthless way. Stress has a lot to do with an inability to dictate circumstances around you – uncertainty, in whatever form it takes, is extremely destabilising. And there was so much uncertainty over this book. I dreaded the reaction from friends and family. Panicked that I'd shot my career in the foot. Couldn't sleep, couldn't shut my brain down at night, felt like my life was imploding. Couldn't finish sentences or complete the simplest tasks – freshly washed clothes were heaped in my sons' bedroom and phone calls went unreturned. I felt as if I was on the edge of a cliff and the silliest thing would push me over. I discovered the horror of migraines for the first time in my life. My life was now held hostage by the feeling that an axe was embedded across my right eyebrow, with brutal regularity.

When the book was published, and took off among readers, the stress only intensified. Of course my publishers wanted me to explain it; the Good Author did what she was told. The Good Author got a bucketing. Often the loudest attackers hadn't read the book. Maybe if they had they would've understood. I said to them back then and I say it now: why don't you attempt to write about sex with a ruthless, unflinching honesty – and put your name to it. All those things you may think but never say, especially to your partner, your friends, your family. It's exhilarating if you're anonymous, but highly traumatic if you're a wife and a mother of two boys, not to mention the daughter of two gently bewildered people in their sixties. And what the naysayers didn't seem understand, in any way, was that anonymity could also arise out of a deep sense of love; a desire not to hurt or confuse people who are cherished. A particular trait of female writers, of course. And so we're back to Virginia, to anonymity being a refuge.

A girlfriend remarked, within the thick of the maelstrom, 'Nikki, you will look back on this time at your grave, and you will laugh.' I couldn't see it then, but gradually, over the years, could. Because what I found in the long run was that honesty connects; that there's an incredible potency to telling the truth. People respond, movingly. It was empowering to have women say things like 'Thank you for writing my words,' or 'Thank you for saying the things I've never been able to articulate.' They did, for years afterwards. In fact still are.

And so it has come to pass. I'm a different woman now, a different writer. Looser, lighter, not so concerned about what people think of me. I found my courage through a book I didn't want anything to do with. It took a long time. My publishers very much wanted a sequel, for this book did well for them. As for me, I wasn't so sure, for years and years afterwards. The problem, or 'challenge', as my rousing editor preferred to see it, was in replicating the feeling of reckless liberation I'd had when writing anonymously. But over a decade I grew up. Let go. Strengthened. Loosened. Didn't give a damn anymore about what people thought of me, and I think that's one of the liberations of middle age. I found my voice. My courage. My boldness. The follow-up came swift and strong and cheeky and sure, just as *Bride* had. Because it's telling the truth, once again. It's got my name on the cover. And it feels great.

Coming home

We emerge from the tube station at Notting Hill Gate into the wan light of early morning. I'm on a brief business trip 'back' to London; my eldest son, aged 11, is accompanying me. And as we climb those scuffed and grotty stars into the morning something extraordinary happens. This boy on the cusp of adulthood loosens away from me, whoops down the street and is gone in a moment from my side. I stare after him – at his exhilaration, his glee, his sheer joy of being alive, here, in this place. And in that moment realise there's a fundamental difference between us: London is in his blood and his bones. He was born in this 'hood, spent the first 10 years of his life here. For him this is not a trip 'back' – but a trip 'home'. Why on earth didn't I see it coming? What am I doing bringing him back into this world so soon after leaving it for good?

A shadow falls across my heart as I stare at his exuberance, his strength here, for I know suddenly, with certainty, that I'll lose him one day to another country, this country. Perhaps forever. He'll always feel the pull of this place in a way I never have. For 14 years I saw this land with outsider's eyes; eyes that were always those of the observer, the interloper, the one who doesn't quite belong. Professionally, I loved that stance; it's the writer's stance where you're never quite comfortable. Personally, it's lonely. But my boy's not lonely here in any way. He's innately an insider and there's a tug of jealousy at that. It's in his walk down this rush hour street, his tallness in it, his ease, delight. He owns this play in a way I never could; moves among these people with authority, as smooth as a shark.

We have lived back in Australia for just over a year and I thought he'd settled completely into his new land, *my* land, but now I wonder. This trip, I fear, will be deeply unsettling for him, open up a chasm between us. In fact I barely see him after the morning arrival; he's stolen by a plethora of childhood mates, passed from one to the other, seized, clamoured over. Some friends inevitably miss out and I'm told off in no uncertain terms by the mothers – but how was I to know that there would be this … enveloping. So strong, so claiming. He is spirited away from me, back into his homeland. Spirited off into the solace of belonging, for seven short days. The tonic of it. And in the brief moments I see him I can tell he's made strong by it.

I never was. No matter how much I revelled in the scruffy dynamism of London – it's scraggy, invigorating, ultimately depleting energy – the great south land always veered my heart. Having children only accelerated the urgency to find a way back for good.

'Stars only happen in videos, Mummy,' my boy had declared knowingly, aged six. It hurt to hear. My little man, born and bred in a metropolis stained by its light pollution, had never properly seen stars, a moon, the vast wondrous canopy of a properly dark, velvety night sky. Never knew what it was like to live under a melodramatic daytime sky of vaulting blue and high cloud. The kids' childhood was all crowded tubes and tiny pocket playgrounds and steely pollution and schools that had little strips of asphalt as their play area, no grass.

Increasingly I had a craving to immerse my brood in the fresh air of my own childhood, in nature, spareness, simplicity; to baste up their little bodies with sunlight. We teach our children to wake up – to the wonder of this world, to its beauty. In Australia nature presses so close, magnificently, you feel the great thumb of it, wear it like a mark. Even in a vast metropolis like Sydney the fecundity is breathtaking when you fly in from dense, crammed, weary, built-over Europe. And as we age, don't we experience an inexorable drawing towards nature? A desire to enfold ourselves back into the sights, smells, sounds of our childhood, when we lived so much closer to the earth, the sky? In London, in the latter years, I'd dreamt nightly of being locked in the sunshine again; of gazing up to that mighty Southern Cross.

After a decade in the Northern world my life was held hostage by a yearning for the sweet, summery air of childhood – for all of us.

'Do not be drawn away from the simplicity of your ancestors,' Gandhi said, and I'd taken that to heart as my Notting Hill life became increasingly complicated by the sheer energy it took just to get by in the place. School runs across three suburbs, endless roadworks, tube breakdowns, bombs scares, tetchy queues, school waiting lists and rain, endless rain – it felt like stress, rush, anxiety was settling around me like concrete. Migraine headaches were becoming a monthly regularity; this was the norm of my life now, escape felt impossible. The weather was becoming harder not easier to bear as the exile years accumulated; the cold in me like grease, sludging me up. I was screaming inside for the WD-40 of sun. I was over the cold, especially the puniness of summer when for three years in a row the clouds of August had never lifted. It was time to be warm again. But how? I couldn't turn to my husband, the chap, the Melbourne man who'd been an Anglophile since childhood.

Despair is about a loss of control. Around the age of 40, I lost it. It felt like I had no say anymore in how I wanted to live, my future; whereas as a single woman I'd had steely, meticulous control over everything in my life: where I lived, how I lived, where I went on holiday, how I looked. I now felt like a housewife from the fifties – drowning, trapped – depression nudging at the corners of my days and blaring me awake at 3am, for hours. Because for the first time in my adult life I wasn't living the life I wanted to, the self-created life. The loss of control, of autonomy, was eating away at my equilibrium, serenity, stillness. I felt weaker in London, less resilient. Craved a life with a lot of quiet in it and wasn't getting it, didn't know how to, didn't think I ever could in this place.

Going home would make me strong again, that's what I thought. But the chap was stalling, stringing out the London years with a succession of buoyant jobs and in the bleakest, darkest times I wondered if he actually wanted a wife like this – broken, weak, pliant – wondered if all men secretly wanted that from their women. I felt unhinged, paranoid, ridiculous.

There was the loneliness, too, because increasingly there was the realisation that I'd never properly belong in this place of exile. In the early days I'd thought there was a chance. But the longer I was in England the more I felt slightly disconnected from the rituals I wasn't completely a part of – the 40th birthdays, christenings, weddings – because with no one was there the bond of blood, with no one was there the rich history stretching back years to childhood, parents, siblings, grandparents.

Every few years my mother would make the trip to us; sometimes she'd stay in our Notting Hill house. Once, as she packed up her room, she asked if she should strip the sheets. 'No,' I said, and smiled. That night I lay in her bed, still stamped with her smell, and deeply slept. Basking just for a night in the certainty of childhood. The simplicity of it, the comfort, the warmth.

Around this time the chap, one day, walked our second son to preschool; on the way our little boy pointed up and said, 'Gummy gum.' The chap gazed up and lo and behold there was a eucalyptus canopy above them (what it was doing in the middle of Notting Hill, I have no idea). He plucked a leaf and crushed it, holding the cup of his palm under his son's nose. 'What does that smell of?' 'In-stralia!' came the joyous reply. The chap laughed. For him, too, it was time. Suddenly, beautifully, miraculously. And curiously he'd come to the decision himself, at a time when I'd stopped the nagging, had just given up. Suddenly, after years of wrangling, the two of us were in alignment. Get the kids away, to a different childhood, a different sky. The prospect for him: a happy wife, which he knew makes a happy home. The prospect for myself: a renovation of my serenity. It was to take us several more years to get home, but we did it.

My eldest boy was 10 by the time we finally extricated ourselves and moved back to Australia permanently. We'd been living under the tall blue sky for just over a year when my son and I embarked on this brief England sojourn. I was curious to know what it would do to my psyche. To my surprise, as the year of return wore on, I was actually missing the great vivid rush of London, its feeling of being firmly at the centre of the world as opposed to the edge of it. Missing the sheer crush of its myriad peoples, missing its great jostling cram of newspapers, magazines, thought. It feels like all the world is in this place.

In comparison, even Australia's largest cities seemed, merely, like big country towns. Sparse. Parochial. Judgmental. Small minded. Consumed by small-town trivialities as opposed to the great roaring breadth of life out there, somewhere else. All around us in our new world are stories of Aussie expats who'd tried to settle back into their homeland but were stung by an eternal restlessness, champing at the bit to return to somewhere else and be among like-minded people again. Some did. Would we? We were warned this England trip would be hugely unsettling – for Lachie. But I knew it might also be for myself.

'My life is one long escape from myself,' Samuel Johnson wrote. Returning home is about confronting yourself; your past, family, friends, the small world you ran from all those years ago. Coming home is about the great circularity of life. I drive the sparse streets of Australia now and think: this is it, for better or for worse – the smallness of it, the intense familiarity – make of it what you will, girl. Both the chap and I are slowing, putting on weight, as we devour the foods from our childhood; within the London energy we were both leaner, faster, uninterested in the confectionary aisles of supermarket because they were sweets we didn't understand. In exile, the craving for return was not something the rational side of me particularly wanted. I needed to stay in

Europe forever, for my career, my contacts, my head told me this. But my heart, blood, bones told me otherwise; they sung me home. I'm back for the solace of home, the solace of belonging. I've given up the fight.

Is my boy showering during his London stay? Brushing his teeth? He's been spirited away by all his mates, he's an 11-year-old boy, I can't get clear answers. I'm the mother who hasn't quite separated yet he's the boy on the cusp of adulthood, and he has. He's returned to me as we leave for Heathrow and the plane journey home. Finally I can talk to him and find out what he's been doing – a day back at his old school; a rain-soaked weekend in Sussex; a trip to the Isle of Wight; a D-Day re-enactment with his best mate, a German boy, 'that no one won'. But his voice sounds different. Over our brief week his newly acquired Australian accent has softened back into its London tones – *swee'ies*, *li'l* – the glottal stop of London street culture. 'I feel torn, Mum,' he says quietly. 'I love Australia but I love here, too.'

The day of return to Australia. The winter weather: 'severe clear'. It's a term used by pilots to denote an infinitely crisp, sunny, blue-sky day. I dreamt of those severe clear days all the years of exile. I look up into the southern sky, and I am found. Know this clearly. My son though? We are fundamentally different. I can't say he's lost, being here in Australia, for he tells me he loves it; he's settled well into his little Aussie primary and within this neighbourhood of kids running into each other's houses and skateboarding down the street and playing cricket on the beach in a way that's old fashioned, affirming, heart-swelling. But when he's in England, *he* is found. It's clear from this trip; obvious and moving and despairing all at once. After a week back in London, immersed in its exuberant energy, I think, no, I couldn't do it again – not with kids. *How* did I do it with kids, for a decade of their little lives? Strollers on tubes, the taste of exhaust fumes in their mouths, school runs that took an hour with the never-ending roadworks.

As I walk the tinlids to school now, along the beach, I think of Prufrock – do I dare to eat a peach? I just want to wear sunshine. Hold my face up to it, slip off my shoes and feel the sand beneath my feet, run down to the water with the kids and fish out the gift of a tennis ball, a hand ball, feel as light-hearted as a child on their first day of holidays. Ah, the great circularity of life. You see, being back in Oz, for better or for worse, I feel righted. This is my lot and I accept it now. I have chosen it and will live with it. Quietly, joyously. It took me a return trip to England to realise it. Nothing is perfect, a part of me will always want London, but I can always visit (most likely, in his adulthood, my eldest son). And as the days wear on in Australia those London glottal stops disappear and the vividness of his life over there recedes; once again, he's immersed in home. *This* home.

A door has opened for me as a writer, and the door is called home. I have to surprise myself again and I'm ready to be surprised by Australia. Hence these columns. This new life, intensely familiar yet wondrous, with its outsider's eyes still. Hence this quiet as I think, observe, note, wonder. I feel as I age my heart is growing young. What is my favourite journey, after all the gypsy years of wandering; all the years of fleeing, escaping, running? For me, now, it is going home.

Lamp lights

Two columns struck a particular resonance with readers – wishes for a new goddaughter, and a follow-up for all those beautiful boys in our lives. The responses were so immediate and heartfelt that I decided to expand the idea, freed from the constraints of newspaper word counts and layouts.

So. A godmother again. What a thrill! All the lovely connotations, not least the deepening of the relationship with the parents in a most profound and trusting way; just as a marriage feels like a deepening between two people who really needn't have bothered with that archaic ritual-thing in this secular day and age, yet do. We have an innate yearning for ritual whether we're religious-minded or not; those ceremonial pauses that charge our life journeys with meaning like a lamp lighter's glow along a darkened path. Yet what does 'godparent' actually mean for so many of us now? I'm no churchgoer, nor is my little Mimosa's family. My own kids have a gloriously mongrel, vivid crew of Christians, Jews and agnostics watching over them – thanks to a rather eccentric, extremely inclusive, and deeply humane Notting Hill vicar who feels to me like the future of the church – yet all the gang, no matter what their beliefs, take the responsibility invested in their role seriously, and with much chuff. It's wonderfully moving. It's about maturing, stepping up to the mark; providing some kind of anchor point in an increasingly jittery, uncentred, Godless world.

The surprising request, binding me most tenderly to little Mosi, arrived alongside a reader's musings on what mothers tell their daughters about life. 'Mine told me nothing. It was as though she thought I had to work it all out for myself … it's a profound area of interest now I have my own daughter. I want her to have an amazing life filled with love, a fearless life.' A wonderful wish and one I hope for all the girls in my life, too. So here, now, are some little lamp lights of observation for the big, wondrous journey ahead of them …

I wish you courage.
Not to dim your light among men. Because so many of us,
    as women, do.
There's pressure to soften so much: our appetites, wants, spark;
    our intelligence, our honesty.
Don't ask anyone for permission to be who you are.

You shape your life, no one else – that is what it means to be
a woman today.

I wish you one true friend.
If you have the solace of that you can forgive all the rest.
I wish you the strength to distance yourself from people
who want to flatten you.
They're not happy, not content, and they'll only want to drag
you down, too.
Cultivate your friends for what's in their heart,
not for how they look or what they do –
or for what they can do for you.

I wish you freedom from fear.
Of what other people think of you, of public opinion.
As George Eliot said, 'It's never too late to be what you might
have been.'
Try, and try again.
I wish you wariness of that reducing little word 'dependent',
for it means letting ourselves be controlled by another person
and there's a whiny unhealthiness in that.
Dependency doesn't breed contentment.
Never underestimate the power of work –
accomplishment makes us happy.

I wish you courage, at some point, to throw away the map.
An appreciation of failure, a respect for it.

Seeing others strive, fail and strive again spurs us all on,
for we're witnessing the glorious, indomitable human spirit
    in action.
I wish you the ability to recognise rupture as an opportunity.
Embrace the unknown, surrender to it.
Dare.

I wish you the strength to respond to your inner voice –
    it's always seeking goodness,
happiness and peace for you.
I wish you that beautifully quiet word, grace.
I wish you the boldness in kindness – the gift of attention,
and a robust sense of empathy.
Curiosity in abundance,
and creativity.
To exhilarate, to still, to nourish.

I wish you bravery.
To be honest. To go against the grain.
To stand up for yourself and for others.
Our lives are made rich by reaching out to those around us,
not by fencing ourselves in with that reducing little word, 'no'.
There are only two ways to live – as a victim or as
    a courageous fighter.
I wish you the blazing latter.
And most fervently, requited love.

A vivid heart. May it never be crushed.
If it is may it love again, fuller, wiser, quieter.

I wish you the solace of the land, close, always;
the replenishing potency of it
like liquid gold through the veins. I wish you tall skies and
    birdsong
and a canopy of green to shade you
and a hurting sun on your back and your face
when you need, achingly, to uncurl,
to thaw from a clenching cold.
I wish you gratitude for the wonders of this ravishingly
    beautiful, constantly surprising world –
a thankful heart.

And finally, for those walloping times of difficulty and doubt,
    I wish you a soldering calm
to know that the bad times dissolve, always.
Lows come into our life for a reason – to enrich us,
to draw us closer into the vast, glittery vividness of what it is to
    be human
and to help us venture back out into the world wiser, softer,
    more compassionate.
In moments of grief and despair and crisis we achieve lucidity.
About who we are,

And where we should go from here.

Be brave, boys

The film *Brave*, that celebration of female empowerment, has all the girls flocking. And the males in it? Stereotypically ridiculous, hot-headed, thuggish, unknowing, vain. Boys get such a hard rap now. It feels like our Western world, still, is in such an uneasy stage of transition in terms of interaction between the sexes; we're still out of balance, trying to work out just how to exist alongside the opposite sex in all its baffling wilfulness, vulnerability and complexity; endlessly grappling with the seismic shock of feminism and the Pandora's box it opened for us.

I celebrate the young men in my life. Yes they're regular rough and tumble boys who love their nerf guns and footy, but alongside that stack the dishwasher and cook and have sensitive, questing conversations about relationships, grown-ups, life. That's what this generation of mothers are teaching their boys, these complex, tender, open and lovely young men who have us roaring with laughter. We can't wait to see how this generation will grow up, how they'll treat women, change the world. But we worry for them too. May they never be crushed, by women most of all, those mocking attitudes increasingly on show in blockbusters like *Brave*. So here they are ... little lamplights of observation for those beautiful, shining boys in our lives.

May you have the soldering fellowship of good,
    reliable mates.
Never be afraid to speak out if you're not happy –
    real mates will support you.
Never underestimate the healing power of a 'man hug',
there's no greater bonding signal.

Keep your head pulled in; tell your friends to pull
    theirs in too if need be.
Impulsive behaviour is often not the best;
thoughtful action gives you leeway to find a better way.
Slow down. Watch. Think.
The world, your team, your peers, may still expect
    a particularly male response –
if that isn't right, don't be that person.
Have the wisdom to know that strength can come
    through tenderness, gentleness,
and that calm resolve will always beat boorish behaviour.
Remember, a gentleman always does the kind thing.

May you never clamp down, shut off, slink away
    into grumpiness.
We women see some little boys bursting with light
    and spark and life,
and then something happens, we're not quite sure what;
a retreat into sullenness, inarticulateness,
the brightness dampened as life chips away at them.

May you have the gift of a male mentor who's not your
    parent;
someone who filters advice you're getting from mates,
tells you what's what, allows you to be emotionally open,
and who steers you through those days of self doubt
    and indecision;
the awakening, the awe.

I wish you'd read as much as you play computer games.
Lift up that beautiful head of yours, gulp the world.
Travel.
Pick a footy team and stick with it through its tough times
    as well as triumphant.
Seize the joy of a physical sport so you can learn to be as
    tough as nails
on the field as it prepares you for the great journey ahead –
and teaches you that getting knocked down
    is all part of life
and getting up again is the real challenge.

I wish you a sense of self that's comfortable rather than
    conformational.
Don't be afraid of eschewing convention, of embracing
    difference,
the 'other'.
Don't cover up your fears with base, herd-like
    behaviour.
Have the courage to be different –
for you may find that by your actions you lead
    by example
and give boys around you someone to follow,
    to look up to.
Don't be afraid to be vulnerable.
It's a close cousin to honesty and people always respond
    to the truth.
Your real self will always know it's false opposite;
don't succumb to it.

I wish you discipline.
Self control.
From that comes great achievements.
Perseverance is the key.
I wish you the ability to love and to articulate it.
Be passionate about what you love and who you love.
Take risks. Have fun. Laugh a lot.
Don't be too serious –
don't be afraid to sing.

And finally, remember that little boy you once were.
May you never, entirely, grow up.
Never lose that joy that sings through you
as you arc across a creek on a tyre, skateboard down a
    path,
whoosh through the surf on a boogie board.
All the women who cherish you are looking at it –
their hearts in their mouths, well, yes –
but giggling at the sheer lovely crazy life affirming
    beauty of it
and wanting you to retain something of it

forever.

Acknowledgments

Thank you to everyone around me who makes my job that little bit easier – at HarperCollins, Anna Valdinger, Belinda Yuille, Christine Farmer and Shona Martyn; and Christine Middap, my editor at the *Weekend Australian Magazine*. Damn impressive the lot of you, and all-round top chicks.

Then there are my esteemed subs at the magazine: Ley Butterworth and Ross Bilton. Thank you for your ingenious headings, warmth and humour, especially when I'm trying to sneak in last-minute changes right on deadline. You save me, again and again.

Thank you to my dear mate, Sue Daniel, for her wonderful photography.

And finally, thank you to the readers who use that email address at the bottom of the columns to send such generous, thoughtful, kind missives. You inspire me to keep going.

The follow-up to The Bride Stripped Bare
WITH MY BODY

Smothered by marriage and family, a woman feels life slipping through her fingers. She becomes preoccupied with thoughts of her early education in love at the hands of Tol, a man like no other she has known. Memories of the affair – Tol's appetite for her pleasure and her trusting desire – consume her. But the mysterious end to their intimacy left her confused and unwilling to love again with all her heart.

Discovering the woman she once was is an erotic journey back into the past, and an exploration of reawakened passion.

'Nikki Gemmell's prose has a wonderful sensuousness'
Independent

'A very knowing, literary erotic romance'
The Australian